Interpretative
Master Planning

Interpretative Master Planning

A Framework for Historical Sites

Elizabeth Nosek

ROWMAN & LITTLEFIELD
Lanham • Boulder • New York • London

Published by Rowman & Littlefield
An imprint of The Rowman & Littlefield Publishing Group, Inc.
4501 Forbes Boulevard, Suite 200, Lanham, Maryland 20706
www.rowman.com

6 Tinworth Street, London SE11 5AL, United Kingdom

British Library Cataloguing in Publication Information Available

Library of Congress Cataloging-in-Publication Data

Names: Nosek, Elizabeth J., 1964- author.
Title: Interpretative master planning : a framework for historical sites / Elizabeth Nosek.
Description: Lanham : Rowman & Littlefield, [2021] | Includes bibliographical references and index. | Summary: "Building on the theories first introduced by Freeman Tilden and the good work done in interpretive planning over the past fifteen years, this book provides the reader with the basics needed for developing a strong interpretive master plan for their institution along with first-hand insights"— Provided by publisher.
Identifiers: LCCN 2021007273 (print) | LCCN 2021007274 (ebook) | ISBN 9781538139240 (cloth) | ISBN 9781538139257 (paperback) | ISBN 9781538139264 (epub)
Subjects: LCSH: Historic sites—Interpretive programs—United States. | Historic sites—United States—Management.
Classification: LCC E159 .N67 2021 (print) | LCC E159 (ebook) | DDC 069/.1—dc23
LC record available at https://lccn.loc.gov/2021007273
LC ebook record available at https://lccn.loc.gov/2021007274

Contents

Acknowledgments

In the early 2000s, while attending a foodways conference at a foodways conference in the mid-Atlantic, I heard a young curator expound on his wonderful, groundbreaking work. He cited his new findings, his revolutionary conclusions, and the "now" correct interpretation of the historic kitchen that was his subject. As he spoke, I realized that not once during his presentation did he mention the fact that none of his findings, his new understanding of the material, or the revolutionary conclusions he had reached would have been possible without the archeologists, historians, curators, volunteers, and—yes—visitors who came before him.

His work did positively impact his museum's interpretation. However, it would not have been possible without all those who preceded him. He stood on their shoulders, and they deserved his thanks.

This book did not come about on its own. It benefitted greatly not only from those who came before me, but from those who have worked beside me throughout my career.

First, I want to thank Charles Harmon and Erin Slanina from Rowman & Littlefield who took a chance on a small museum curator in Colorado. They not only checked my grammar, but pushed me to make my work better. Next, few people are lucky enough to have knowledgeable friends who can be trusted to look at your rough drafts objectively, pushing you to think deeper. Kris Autobee is one such friend. She not only helped me make this book better, but ensured the process was fun. I am fortunate to know her and even luckier to be her friend. Tom Kelleher, another trusted and longtime friend, gave me honest and wise counsel as always. I am especially indebted to him for helping me navigate some political waters along the way. Still another friend and peer, Stephanie Gilmore, not only proofed one of my rough drafts, but patiently listened to and commented on some of the ideas I developed for the book's content.

Inspiration came from many directions, including the staff, volunteers, and stakeholders involved in the Colorado Railroad Museum's interpretive master planning process, particularly executive directors Donald Tallman and Paul Hammond, as well as our consultant, Conservation by Design's Melanie Pierson.

The opportunity to discuss interpretive planning with many of my colleagues across the United States was one of the perks of this project. All of my colleagues shared information that helped to inform my writing, even if not specifically included in this book. Special thanks go to interpretive planners: Katie Boardman, Jenny Rigby, Rici Peterson, Melanie Pierson, and Lisa Brochu, whose books, interviews, conversations, and examples further strengthened my perspective on and understanding of the process of interpretive planning. It is on their shoulders that I am privileged to stand.

This book's appendixes include five case studies from the House of the Seven Gables, the Silos and Smokestacks National Heritage Area, the Cumbres and Toltec Scenic Railroad, Old Sturbridge Village, and 'Iolani Palace. My interviews with my colleagues at these organizations were enlightening. I found each of my peers to be open about the good and not-so-good experiences of developing and implementing their plans. Not only did each approach their own interpretive master plans in a slightly different manner, but each planning process's final product was unique to their own institution. Thank you Julie Arrison-Bishop of the House of the Seven Gables, Candy Welch-Streed of Silos and Smokestacks National Heritage Area, John Bush of the Cumbres and Toltec Scenic Railroad, Caitlin Emery Avenia and Tom Kelleher of Old Sturbridge Village, and Teresa Valencia of 'Iolani Palace. This book is richer for your contributions.

I would be remiss not to express my love and appreciation for my family, who threatened me with an embroidered pillow stating, "I can't, I am working on the book." This book would not have been possible without their patience and support.

Last but not least are my friends, family, and peers who are allowing me to use their images for the book. This book is a richer experience because of you, thank you!

Each person mentioned inspired me and helped me to refine my understanding of just what interpretation was, and could be, when developed from the basis of an interpretive master plan. Please know that I am the better for it, and the help was greatly appreciated.

And of course, thank you, Freeman Tilden!

Preface

I hope to touch people's lives and make a difference. I believe in embracing opportunities to share my love of museums and their treasures. I revel in using interpretation to help visitors make connections. I look for openings that stretch my own understanding of interpretation. I honor those who came before me as I build on their efforts and share my knowledge in turn. These are a few of the reasons I decided to write *Interpretative Master Planning: A Framework for Historical Sites*.

HOW I CAME TO WRITE THIS BOOK

While I can honestly lay claim to such virtuous reasons for writing this book, there is another, much more mundane story behind how this particular book came to be.

Writing a book has been on my bucket list for quite a while. The actual opportunity to do so came in New Orleans at the American Alliance of Museums Annual Meeting in May 2019. My own museum had just undertaken development of our own interpretive master plan, and I was determined to learn everything I could to ensure our plan would not just meet our needs, but exceed them. I was searching for current books on the subject at the American Alliance of Museums' bookstore, conveniently located in the convention hall. I was not very successful in finding what I needed when I was introduced to my soon-to-be editor, Charles Harmon. After speaking briefly about my own museum's interpretive master plan project and my efforts to find resources to help me ensure we created the strongest possible plan for our institution, Charles suggested that maybe I should consider writing the book I was looking for and encouraged me to send him a proposal. I did, and was under contract by September.

Once started, it didn't take me long to discover that writing a book is a lot of work. But I told myself to buck up, most worthwhile things are . . . and I really wanted to make a difference and offer something of worth to a profession I love.

I also came to understand that there were a lot of people who wanted to be writing this book. This came to my attention when I shared that I was working on a book about interpretive master planning, and this was followed by a meaningful pause. More often than not, the person I was speaking with had as much or more experience on the subject than I. It was at this point that I learned a few very important lessons: (1) My experience has worth, and (2) I work in an incredibly generous field with colleagues who are willing to share their experiences, viewpoints, and wisdom. This is just one of the many reasons that I love museums and the work they do.

I began this project with the understanding that I cannot possibly incorporate everything about interpretive master planning into a single book. What I can do is to provide a slightly different perspective, and that is the perspective of one in the trenches. As a museum curator, I undertook my museum's interpretive master plan not only because I needed it to do my job, but saw how my coworkers struggled without a consistent interpretive message. I found the funding, defined what was needed in a consultant, and put together the team that could build the support needed to make our plan successful. I bought cookies, sharpened pencils, and did whatever else it took to ensure that at the end of the day, we had a plan that provided the framework on which our museum could grow.

THE CHAPTERS

Like many museum professionals who saw a need for an interpretive master plan, I wasn't quite sure at first just how to communicate its importance to both my coworkers and our museum board. Chapters 1 and 2 help do just that. The first, "Just What Is Interpretation?" explains the basics of interpretation and its place among the various core planning documents within an institution. The second, "Are You Ready to Create an Interpretive Master Plan?" looks at the work that goes into just getting ready to plan. Reviewing institutional documents, finding funds to support the planning process, and building support among your leadership are all necessary steps preparing you to dive into the formal planning process. Chapter 2 also discusses two approaches to interpretive planning that have evolved over time: interpretation as an art form; and a more systematic approach favored by nature centers and park systems and championed by the National Association for Interpretation.

Chapter 3, "Self-Study/Research," lays out the necessary work needed before the focus groups and brainstorming may commence. A review of an organization's institutional history, and an examination of existing core documents such as the mission statement and vision, provide good stepping stones to understanding an organization's message and even its underlying values. The self-study also looks at the museums collection's strengths and weaknesses as well as reviews existing programming. For an even better understanding of itself, a museum's self-study should explore the surrounding community by looking at regional demographics, similar institutions, and surveying its visitors for their perspectives on the museum's message.

Chapter 4, "Creating Your Team," leads the reader through the process of identifying and bringing together those individuals best qualified to lead your organization through an interpretive planning process. Interpretive master planning is a collaborative affair, but one that includes specific roles to move the project forward in the manner best suited to a particular institution. This chapter explores how to select stakeholders with a broad range of experiences, and goes on to identify the three leadership roles that lead to a successful project: the coordinator, the champion, and the guide.

Chapter 5, "Facilitating Focus Groups," is a response to a request from a colleague with whom I discussed the book. She wanted ideas for working with groups and keeping creative juices flowing during brainstorming sessions. Facilitating a meeting is not often recognized as the art it is. It is not a skill that comes naturally to everyone, but a skill that needs to be developed over time and occasionally refreshed. The chapter offers a few commonsense suggestions and techniques learned over the years.

Chapter 6 on "Defining Themes" for your museum's interpretation is at the very heart of any interpretive master plan. It follows, then, that this chapter is essential. In my own museum's planning experience, there were a number of discussions on just what a good interpretive theme is. Good interpretive themes are complete thoughts—relevant, concise, provocative, and meaningful. They are not topics, titles, slogans, soundbites, headlines, questions, or commands. Most importantly, an interpretive theme's ultimate goal is to provoke its audiences into thinking and developing their own points of view. This is not as simple to do as it may seem. A lot of attention is given to this process in other books about interpretive planning. To help facilitate the process, I used a theme statement exercise that many may remember experiencing in high school English classes.

Chapter 7, "Putting It All Together—Writing the Plan," considers how to actually put all the work done to this point down on paper. A written plan is unique to each institution, and as the end product it records and prioritizes the choices made and analyzes the factors that went into making those choices. It also creates a path for the museum as a whole to follow in order to achieve greater success.

The final chapter of the book, "Creating a Plan for Implementation," looks at how to implement the interpretive master plan by using a matrix that identifies the various projects in the plan and placing these into a timeline based on the necessary staff, costs, resources, and evaluation methods to carry these out. The Colorado Railroad Museum's experience in addressing the COVID-19 pandemic is used to illustrate how the museum was able to use their interpretive master planning experience to help them to adjust to changing times and needs in their world.

One of my favorite portions of the book is the appendixes that cover five interpretive master plan case studies. Each case study represents a different type of organization, time in the organization's interpretive development, institutional size, and geographic location, as well as a range of underlying reasons for developing an interpretive master plan in the first place. Using interviews with my professional counterparts, their institutions' interpretive master plans, and other supporting documents as available, I was able to provide a window into their experiences developing and using interpretive master plans. Hopefully, this will prove helpful to others looking for a better understanding of not only what it takes to create an interpretive master plan, but also how a plan can support an institution's growth.

The case studies provide ample opportunity for comparison. Some plans exceeded their institution's expectations; others were thrown out. A number of plans incorporated the histories of people previously ignored, with surprisingly mixed success. The audiences identified varied from organization to organization. A number of plans highlighted families as well as people of color. Some chose to focus on baby boomers, while others decided to try to attract millennials through their programming. Regardless of their similarities or differences, each case study developed an interpretive master plan that they thought fit their unique needs.

Interpretive master planning is arguably a field filled with experts. In fact, it was specifically because I wasn't an expert on interpretive master planning that I believe my voice might prove somewhat unique amid the chorus. The result is a framework that includes the basics of interpretation and the evolution of interpretive planning, as well as the roles needed to develop an interpretive master plan. This book discusses the basics required for self-study, group facilitation, and theme development. It updates readers on available resources that can support them throughout the process of interpretive planning. It points out just how important it is to develop a plan that the whole organization can get behind. Most importantly, *Interpretative Master Planning: A Framework for Historical Sites* provides a perspective that readers working on the front lines in museums can relate to as they endeavor to engage their visitors.

Chapter One

Just What Is Interpretation?

One of my best friends is fond of saying, "A good relationship is one in which the structure is well-defined." She was talking about human relationships such as those between an employer and employee, husband and wife, and, yes, even friends. Over the years, I have often been struck by just how broadly this statement can be taken. I use it often myself, but a "structure that is well-defined" is sometimes switched out with, "built upon a strong foundation."

A good foundation and well-defined structure are important in pretty much every aspect of life. When you purchase a home, you expect it to be set on a strong foundation with a water-tight roof that will protect you and your family from harm when storms rage outside. Parents tell their children to get a good education because they believe it will provide the foundation that will lead to a successful career. And employers look at the college degrees listed on an applicant's resume as well as their work experience to help determine if the applicant fits within the hiring organization's structure. Teachers work diligently to create classroom environments that help foster learning among their students. And we trust and rely on our friends, with whom we have laid a foundation of kindness, empathy, and honesty, as we endure the bad times and celebrate the good.

Over the last 50 years, museums and similar cultural organizations have also been laying their own foundational system. Recognizing that they need strong foundations, sturdy walls, and weatherproof roofs, they have embraced the idea of institutional planning. In fact, over 18 different planning documents have been identified by the American Alliance of Museums.

Of these, the American Alliance of Museums considers a strategic institutional plan, disaster preparedness and emergency response plan, and a collections management policy to be an institution's core documents.[1] Of these documents, perhaps the one most familiar to us is the master plan; also known

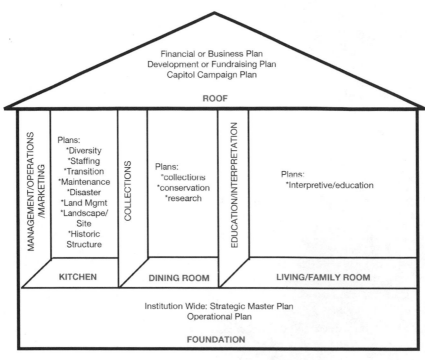

Figure 1.1.   Planning for a Good Foundation Diagram. Photo courtesy of author

as a strategic, institutional, or long-range plan. This mission-based document creates a vision of the organization's future and incorporates all the museum's various departments. The American Alliance of Museums provides this definition for a master plan:

> A strategic institutional plan (often referred to as a strategic plan or long-range plan) is a document that is multi-year, aligned with the museum's mission, and contains measurable goals and methods by which the museum can evaluate success. A plan should be current and aligned with the museum's mission. A strong plan includes prioritized action steps, establishes timelines, and assigns responsibilities for implementing the plan. It also assesses and addresses the resources needed to see the plan to fruition.[2]

Many institutions leave well enough alone. After all, a master plan provides that all-important foundation (figure 1.1). Ideally, it communicates an overall vision for its organization to pursue and a plan for how to pursue that vision. However, not all organizations end up with a strategic plan that provides a blueprint that includes interpretation. (In fact, not all museums clearly understand interpretation, and why it is an essential part of any museum's strategy for success.) What does an interpretive master plan offer that the scope of a strategic institutional plan does not? An interpretive master plan strengthens an institution's strategic master plan by integrating interpretive themes that engage its audience(s) with the museum's mission.

Like homes, careers, classrooms, and friends; museum interpretation is best when built within a structure that supports it. At its most basic level, an interpretive master plan provides the structure for an organization's interpretive programming. Like all planning documents, if it is done well, it will stand the test of time. Done poorly, at best it will sit on a shelf, collecting dust, unappreciated and ignored.

We can fill out that definition a bit more by looking at how interpretive planning came into being. First, we need to consider interpretation. What is it? Recently, the host at a restaurant where I had lunch asked me what "historic interpreter" meant. After I explained, he smiled and said, "Oh I always thought it had to do with foreign languages."

There have been a number of definitions for interpretation over the years. In fact, the National Association of Interpretation produced a fun YouTube video in 2014 entitled, "I Am an Interpreter." They filmed various interpreters from a wide array of organizations around the world discussing their definitions of what interpretation is and what it does. The most common words and phrases cropping up over and over in the footage are "building connections," "care," "facilitate," "help," "sense of self," and "place."[3]

Three other words that popped up in the "I Am An Interpreter" video were "provoke," "relate," and "reveal."[4] These words entered the interpretive lexicon when Freeman Tilden's book, *Interpreting Our Heritage*, was first published in 1957.[5] At that time the book proved to be a lightning rod, spurring on the concept of planned interpretation for museums, state and national parks, botanical gardens, and like cultural organizations around the world. Today, it remains the primary text for professional interpretation upon which all other interpretive works are built. Tilden did not lay out directions for creating an interpretive plan, but he did review the tours, exhibits, and signage of the museums and parks of his era. He applied that information to extrapolate the basic principles of interpretation that are still in use today. And while Tilden did not coin the term "interpretation," his book made it a household word—in the world of museums, historic sites, parks, aquariums, and gardens. Today, *Interpreting Our Heritage* and its six principles of interpretation are considered a foundational work (textbox 1.1).

TEXTBOX 1.1 TILDEN'S SIX PRINCIPLES OF INTERPRETATION

1. Any interpretation that does not somehow relate what is being displayed or described to something within the personality or experience of the visitor will be sterile.
2. Information, as such, is not Interpretation. Interpretation is revelation based upon information. But they are entirely different things. However, all interpretation includes information.
3. Interpretation is an art, which combines many arts, whether the materials presented are scientific, historical or architectural. Any art is in some degree teachable.
4. The chief aim of Interpretation is not instruction but provocation.
5. Interpretation should aim to present a whole rather than a part, and must address itself to the whole man rather than any phrase.
6. Interpretation addressed to children (say, up to the age of twelve), should not be a dilution of the presentation to adults, but should follow a fundamentally different approach. To be at its best it will require a separate program.[6]

While interpretation has been in existence for as long as people have been telling stories, and Tilden's six principles provided the structure by which we began to develop interpretive programming, the concept of interpretive master planning is relatively new. Born during the mid-twentieth century, interpretive planning was a response to federal legislation that required public input into how public lands were managed by federal agencies such as the Bureau of Land Management, the U.S. Forest Service, and the National Park Service (NPS).[7]

It was the National Park Service's publication of the *Interpretive Planning Handbook* in 1965 that first outlined a process to look at what programs, facilities, and media were needed to communicate a park or historic site's message to its visitors.[8] It also identified objectives and considered the various consequences—both positive and negative—that the plan could have. These early planners believed such a study would help management make informed decisions about the programs and facilities the park or historic site needed or desired. At that time, Bill Everhart, the assistant director of Interpretation for the Park Service, authorized the establishment of guidelines for interpretive planning, writing "The purpose of interpretive planning is to establish a climate of creativity and innovation in which the broad talents of park interpreter, and the specialized talents of the AV [audiovisual] producer, the exhibit designer, and the publication specialist, can be utilized in ever-changing combinations, as the situation demands."[9]

In her thesis, "Practice-Based Perspectives on the Interpretive Planning Process," Leonor A. Colbert defined interpretive plans as "living documents and decision-making aids used by museum professionals when developing persuasive and relatable visitor experiences." She goes on to discuss how interpretive plans "can be utilized in a variety of scales, from plans for programs or exhibits to comprehensive or long-range interpretive master plans that encompass the entire institution."[10] This is a relatively new take on the more comprehensive interpretive master plan. It allows institutions to support the validity of new (and increasingly expensive) programs and exhibits by ensuring the project's relevance. Whatever an interpretive project's size, it must engage the visitor. To do this, it must not only make sense, and be fun, but also be based on sound research. Typical interpretive plans, whether for the entire institution or a more specific project such as an exhibit, will always be tied to the museum's mission statement. Furthermore, these plans will focus on a specific idea and define one or more specific audiences toward which to target their communication.

In 2018, 54 years after the publication of the first edition of the Park Service's *Interpretive Planning Handbook*, in my capacity as the curator of education and exhibits for the Colorado Railroad Museum, I wrote a grant to enable my institution to develop an interpretive master plan. The grant defined the proposed plan as follows:

> An Interpretive Master Plan is a strategic planning document that provides clear guidelines for creating seamless, consistent, enjoyable and relevant experiences for the visitor. It analyzes visitor demographics and the overall visitor experience, crafts an interpretive vision, develops interpretive goals (longer-term achievements), and defines the messages the Museum wishes to convey through its educational programming. It recommends and prioritizes measurable action steps to achieve identified goals. A plan should also examine site operations as they relate to the visitor experience including visitor welcome and ticketing, safety/security, website, wayfinding, visitor amenities, and hospitality.
>
> Through evaluating these areas, an interpretive master plan can determine the approaches which are best for its messages and audience. It can identify barriers to the visitor's experience, as well as developing interpretation recommendations that convey a few clear, consistently reinforced interpretive themes.
>
> An interpretive plan identifies existing exhibits and spaces that need updating and provides a solid foundation for initiating new projects. By prioritizing these projects for the entire institution, the plan helps ensure that money and effort are used efficiently and effectively.[11]

Founded in 1958, the Colorado Railroad Museum is a privately run, small nonprofit railroad museum averaging 12 to 14 full-time staff and 300 volunteers. Governed by a dedicated board passionate about its subject matter, in 2020 the organization arrived at the end of a 10-year strategic master plan focusing on collecting and restoring railcars. Board members, staff, and volunteers throughout the museum—collections and archives, the roundhouse (where restorations are done), education, exhibits, volunteers, and visitor services, were all with the best of intentions making decisions on which themes and priorities would be emphasized. Not all of these choices were consistent with those being made by their colleagues, nor were they being effectively communicated. In fact, in some situations, the decisions made confused our visitors and volunteers about what and who we were.

I attempted to address the issue, at least in part, with an interpretive manual. The ensuing staff/volunteer feedback made it apparent that all our jobs would be easier if we had an overarching plan that took into account the visitor experience. We needed more input from our community, volunteers, staff, and board to determine what messages we were presenting to our public. For the museum to move forward, it was vital that we determine a cohesive message—not only for our visitors, but also for ourselves. The foundation for our messaging should be our interpretive theme(s). An interpretive master plan would set forth a structure around which all departments could work. Interpretation should inform and be informed by the work being done in all areas of the museum, including collections, guest service, marketing, development, and education.

Again, I sought a way to address our need, and found an education grant offered by Colorado's State Historic Fund for Preservation. It provided our institution with funding that enabled us to write an interpretive master plan that gathered the necessary input and defined a set of overarching interpretive themes.

In the research for writing my grant, I looked at other institutions that had undergone the process and why they had seen this as a worthy project. I also looked at how they had approached the process of interpretive planning and, finally, the benefits they derived from the plan.

I found an impressive PowerPoint created by the Nova Scotia Museum in Canada. Now on the web, "True Confessions about Interpretive Master Planning" was first presented at the International Interpretation Conference. Among the reasons for needing an interpretive master plan, the Nova Scotia Museum cited dropping visitor numbers, the museum isolated from its communities, weak interpretive capacity, changing visitor expectations, the too-narrow scope of stories being told, and to the desire to better leverage resources.[12]

The U.S. Forest Service's Center for Design and Interpretation also lists a number of reasons for wanting to pursue an interpretive master plan, and many of these struck a chord as reasons why my institution and many others chose to pursue an interpretive plan. Conducting all interpretive efforts independent of each other, with no continuity or evaluation of needs based on area or forest goals, is a natural result of not having a cohesive plan. The need to improve the Forest Service's public image, and create consistency in its key messages and communication strategies, is an underlying tenet of not only museums, but any business's success. A desire to improve the public's understanding of, and appreciation for, the resources of national forests and why they are managed the way they are furthers the institutional message. The Forest Service's desire to improve public involvement, garner new partnerships, and promote community commitment to public lands management is integral to any nonprofit's success. The Forest Service also recognized the agency's continuing need to develop a heightened sense of individual stewardship. As is too often the case, current interpretive, educational, and informational service programs lack adequate funding, prioritization, or integration. And finally, the Forest Service wanted to support its staff with a new tool that could assist them in recruiting partners in interpretation.[13]

Interpretive specialists who consult in the field developed a variety of approaches to interpretive planning as they moved into the twenty-first century. While each offers a unique approach, these methods also have a great deal in common, as they were all built upon Freeman Tilden's six principles of interpretation and the National Park Service's original *Interpretive Planning Handbook*. The National Park Service's *Planning for Interpretation and Visitor Experience* (1998) and *Comprehensive Interpretive Planning* (2000) build on this earlier work. The California State Parks System's *Interpretation Planning Workbook* (2013) offers a systematic approach to interpretive planning, reflecting the bureaucracy necessary for a state with the fifth-largest economy in the world. John Veverka, author of *Interpretive Master Planning* (2011), is by far the most prolific among the authors mentioned here. He continually updates his work through his website in an effort to stay current with the needs of our profession. *Interpretive Planning for Museums: Integrating Visitor Perspectives in Decision Making* by Marcella Wells, Barbara Butler, and Judith Koke (2013) is a classic in this area. The National Association of Interpretation built its program for interpretive planning on *Interpretive Planning: The 5-M Model for Successful Planning Projects* by Lisa Brochu (2014).

For her thesis, Colbert interviewed seven professional interpretive planners (three of whom authored texts mentioned in the prior paragraph) to better understand the difference between what the literature recommended the process of creating an interpretive plan should be and the reality of what the experience actually turned out to be. According to her informants, no interpretive planning experience is the same, and no single best practice exists. That said,

Colbert identified several recurring themes and developed the following "key practices and values"[14] that agreed with my own understanding of what my museum would want to undertake as best practices for interpretive planning:

1. Interpretive planning is systematic. Its methodology should be transparent to those questioning its validity.
2. Interpretive planning values interpretive principles, including meaning, provocation, and engagement. Tilden remains as relevant today as he was in 1957.
3. Interpretive planning is a visitor-focused practice. It remains imperative that we understand and listen to our audiences.
4. Interpretive planning requires continual consensus building. In order for people to buy into any plan, they must feel that their voices have been heard.
5. Decisions made throughout the interpretive planning process are evidence-based and require in-depth analysis of information gathered from a variety of sources. This takes the process to the next level by supporting the thoughts and ideas gathered from focus groups with documentation on area demographics, site history, and actual resources available.

A lot has changed since the National Park Service's first *Interpretive Planning Handbook* in 1965. Today, interpretation is seen as a central building block for programming, and we have a wider range of technological tools at our disposal that should be incorporated into our planning documents. The majority of Americans have visited some type of museum, and expect those institutions to cater to more of their wants and needs. To do that, organizations need their input. No longer are museums seen as a depository for a bunch of old stuff or pretty pictures. Parks cannot exist as wildlife refuges alone. Visitors want more than a "talk at and drag around" tour. They want authentic experiences that engage and enlighten. Visitor expectations for meaningful experiences herd these cultural institutions toward new roles where they must act in concert with the visitor. An interpretive master plan can help a museum define what that role is for their institution. It can provide a foundation on which to build a rich and engaging experience.

NOTES

1. American Alliance of Museums, "Core Documents," AAM Ethics, Standards, and Professional Practices, accessed August 28, 2019, https://www.aam-us.org/programs/ethics-standards-and-professional-practices/core-documents/.

2. American Alliance of Museums, "Developing a Strategic Institutional Plan," AAM Alliance Reference Guide, 2018, https://www.aam-us.org/wp-content/uploads /2017/12/Developing-a-Strategic-Institutional-Plan-2018.pdf.

3. NAIinterpret, "I Am an Interpreter," YouTube, August 18, 2014, video, 3:00, https://www.youtube.com/watch?v=8kZe5NosGxo.

4. Ibid.

5. Freeman Tilden, *Interpreting Our Heritage*, third ed. (Chapel Hill: University of North Carolina Press, 1987).

6. Ibid., 9.

7. Marcella Wells, Barbara Butler, and Judith Koke, *Interpretive Planning for Museums: Integrating Visitor Perspectives in Decision Making* (Walnut Creek, CA: Left Coast Press, Inc. 2013), 32.

8. National Park Service, *Interpretive Planning Handbook* (Harper's Ferry Center, WV: U.S. Department of the Interior, 1982), http://npshistory.com/publications/inter pretation/interp-planning-handbook-1982.pdf.

9. Ibid., 17.

10. Leonor A. Colbert, "Practiced-Based Perspectives on the Interpretive Planning Process," (master's thesis, University of Washington, 2017), 1, https://digital.lib .washington.edu/researchworks/handle/1773/39766.

11. Elizabeth J. Nosek, State Historic Fund Education Grant, Colorado Railroad Museum Interpretive Master Plan—Education, 2018.

12. Nova Scotia Museum, "True Confessions about Interpretive Master Planning: An Interactive Session," Slide Share, May 2, 2015, slide 6, https://www.slideshare.net /mags_x/true-confessions-about-interpretive-master-planning-a-presentation-by-the -nova-scotia-museum-for.

13. U.S. Forest Service, Center for Design and Interpretation, *Interpretive Planning—Tool #2: Interpretive Plans*, Version 2 (Golden, CO: USDA Forest Service, September 2014), 1.

14. Colbert, "Practiced-Based Perspectives on the Interpretive Planning Process," 45.

Chapter Two

Are You Ready to Create an Interpretive Master Plan?

In preparing for battle I have always found that plans are useless, but planning is indispensable.

—Dwight D. Eisenhower

Before the consultants are hired and stakeholders invited, it is the educator, interpreter, and curator who come to the realization that they don't have the tools they need to be truly successful. More direction is needed to provide the inspiration vital to building connections between the information held in the collections and the visitor walking through the door. To create successful programming, we need to understand just what it is about our museum that provides the spark to move our message forward. Or, in the spirit of Tilden, we need to create interpretation that does not instruct, but provokes—interpretation that does not stand on its own, sterile and meaningless, but relates to visitors' current lives and experiences.

More often than not, it is the educators who start the push for interpretive planning. Educators are the ones who are doing the heavy lifting in this area, after all. Once they realize there are pieces of the puzzle missing, it is in their nature and training to look for the pieces and fit them into place. A friend and I attended one of the Denver area's first Museum Educators' Roundtable in the 1990s. On leaving what was supposed to be a single meeting, I expressed my surprise that we had a full slate of educational programming for the coming year. This group of strangers had put a year's worth of programming together in about an hour. My friend turned to me and said with a smile, "What do you expect? Put a bunch of museum educators in a room and within 20 minutes they will more than likely develop a program schedule on some topic or another. There is just too much creativity in the room not to." I have

experienced this phenomena time and again. It is innate. We just can't seem
to help ourselves.

Which makes it all the more surprising that some of my museum colleagues are pushing back against the idea of interpretive planning, even as
they read this. I get it—there are many reasons why those of us creating the
tours, exhibits, and other programs wouldn't want to take the time to come up
with a plan. Anyone in our profession knows that we wear many hats. It isn't
unusual for a single employee to handle exhibits, education, and volunteers.
Or collections, exhibits, and the store. Or marketing, exhibits, and . . . well,
you get the idea; the combinations are endless. Whatever the combination,
each of those hats takes up a good deal of time and energy. In fact, colleagues
from small and mid-sized museums cite the multiple hats they wear when
interpretive planning is suggested, and they respond with the infamous, "I
don't have time," or "It gets in the way of my real work." My question is, Do
you have time *not* to?

In 2008, the then American Association of Museums (AAM; now the
American Alliance of Museums) published *National Standards and Best
Practices for U.S. Museums*. Planning is cited as a main component of professional standards, and has its own section alongside Mission, anticipating
a process that includes board, staff, and stakeholders.[1] Though this section of
the book focuses on institutional planning, many of the same standards can be
referenced for interpretive planning as well. AAM has long recognized that
it is the plan that keeps the organization's programming going in the right
direction and leverages the necessary support to help it grow.

INTERPRETIVE PLANNING TRADITIONS

At least two schools of thoughts have evolved since Freeman Tilden first
defined interpretation as "an educational activity, which aims to reveal meanings and relationships through the use of original objects, by firsthand experience, and by illustrative media, rather than simply to communicate factual information."[2] The two traditions can be loosely defined as a humanities school
of thought used by many historic sites and museums, and the more structured
path favored by nature centers and parks (table 2.1). Both traditions cite Tilden and his six principles of interpretation as the basis for their practice as
interpreters. They also point to the National Park Service as the origin of their
understanding of interpretation. However, their approaches vary. Museums
emphasizing what Tilden called the "art of interpretation," like nature centers
and parks, follow a more systematic approach.

Table 2.1.   Interpretive Planning Traditions

	Traditional Museums	*National Association of Interpretation*
Origin	Freeman Tilden and the National Park Service	Freeman Tilden and the National Park Service
Nomenclature	See interpretation as part of education	See education as part of interpretation
What interpretive plans look like	Every site is unique with its own challenges and opportunities	There is no template for interpretive planning
Interpretive planners Background	Use personal experience and training to develop an individual approach to interpretive planning. They rely on professional standards set out by the American Alliance of Museums for education.	Utilize certification program to train planners. These certified planners have been reviewed by peers, proven competent, and participate in ongoing training. They then use the models they were taught to develop their own approach in working with clients.
Terminology for interpretive planners	Consultant, museum professional	Interpretive planners, consultant
Approach to interpretive planning	Traditionally focused on collections and education to engage visitors	Heavily influenced by nature centers and park systems approach
Terminology used for interpreters	Docent, guide, host, interpreter	Host, guide, interpreter
Interpreter focus	Object, story/theme, hands-on activities, relevance to visitor	Interactives/hands-on activities and themes, relevance to visitor
Viewed from the outside as	Very fluid Focusing on the breadth and nuances that take interpretation to the level of an art form Structured to follow the visitor by providing information and resources that enhance the experience offered by objects	Worthy of respect Highly structured with lots of rubrics and formulas to be followed Structured to provide information and interactive resources for visitors to follow in order to understand the story being told

John Falk and Lynn Dierking revolutionized how we looked at our visitors and sparked a new age of engagement in interpretation with their book *The Museum Experience*, first published in 1992. This has evolved further in the current era by emphasizing experience design. Now both museums and nature centers and parks are looking even deeper for opportunities to involve visitors in interpreting their stories. There appears to be more and more overlap between these two traditions as those involved in interpretive master planning take advantage of and adapt the tools of both traditions to suit their needs.

In over 30 years as an interpreter, educator, and curator, my work never suffered because I took time out to plan at the front end of a project. In fact, the more time I invested upfront to ensure a plan was in place, the better the program, exhibit, or experience was for visitors and staff alike. Like most museum professionals, I have a few program skeletons in my closet. In each and every case, a bit more time spent on the plan at the start of the project would have alleviated the issue, if not completely solved it.

Another issue programmers have with planning is their concern that it might confine them and their creativity. In fact, the opposite is true. Creativity breeds more creativity and provides further resources for your project. Let's return for a moment to our foundation metaphor in chapter 1. A strong foundation and clear blueprints don't limit the interior designer's work. Rather, a foundation becomes the clean slate on which the designer can build a dynamic environment in which the homeowner will live.

There are still those who want to do it all themselves, and they can be successful, but uncountable opportunities are lost for making the most of their idea(s). No one takes a museum job so that they don't have to think or use their ingenuity. In fact, experience has taught me that planning not only *doesn't* limit our ability to be creative, but actually creates the space to foster creativity.

KNOW YOUR GOAL

Before you commit to undertaking an interpretive master plan, it is worth taking some time to reflect on your goals and how to measure them. You need to ask yourself: What are you hoping to accomplish? What results do you want to see? How will an interpretive plan move your organization forward? Does your museum staff and board understand what cultural interpretation is? The first chapter of this book provided all sorts of reasons museums create interpretive plans. What are yours? If you can't clearly articulate your reasons and convey them to your board, director, fellow staff, and volunteers—you aren't ready. Without a clear end goal, an interpretive planning process is a waste of your time. You will just be spinning your wheels.

For me, I wanted to stop throwing spaghetti at the wall to see what stuck. Each program, exhibit, and event was a guess as to what visitors might find interesting enough to support. Without a plan, it was difficult to determine what and who the institution as a whole wanted to emphasize. Here is how I articulated our end goal in the education grant for our museum:

[The museum] has now arrived at a crossroads where an overarching plan is essential for continuing the stewardship of its compelling and extensive railroad collection and dynamic programming. By acting as a decision making tool, an Interpretive Master Plan will serve to preserve and interpret the museum's railroad collection balancing management requirements and resource considerations with visitors' wants and needs.[3]

In the *National Standards and Best Practices for U.S. Museums*, the section "Education and Interpretation" discusses a range of standards from program quality to evaluation, intellectual rigor, audiences, and physical and intellectual accessibility to interpretive planning (see textbox 2.1). At first glance, these standards can seem overwhelming. But striving toward a high standard ensures excellence, so all these ideas are worth keeping in mind not only when you are developing programming, but when you are planning.

TEXTBOX 2.1 NATIONAL STANDARDS AND BEST PRACTICES FOR U.S. MUSEUMS

Standards Regarding Education and Interpretation:

- The museum clearly states its overall educational goals, philosophy and messages, and demonstrates that its activities are in alignment with them.
- The museum understands the characteristics and needs of its existing and potential audiences and uses this understanding to inform its interpretation.
- The museum's interpretive content is based on appropriate research.
- Museums conducting primary research do so according to scholarly standards.
- The museum uses techniques, technologies and methods appropriate to its educational goals, content, audiences and resources.

- The museum presents accurate and appropriate content for each of its audiences.
- The museum demonstrates consistent high quality in its interpretive activities.
- The museum assesses the effectiveness of its interpretive activities and uses those results to plan and improve its activities.[4]

KNOW YOUR PLANS

It is also important to think about where your institution is in the development of its core documents. These five documents (mission statement, institutional code of ethics, strategic institutional plan, disaster preparedness and emergency response plan, and a collections management policy) are considered "core" documents, as they create an underlying base for professional museum operations that at the same time exemplifies core museum values and practices. This chapter adds the organization's mission statement and its institutional code of ethics to the list of core planning documents mentioned in chapter 1. Both the mission statement and code of ethics act as the foundational base for all the other planning documents. Having these basic documents in place provides a framework on which to build a strong interpretive master plan.

While ideal, this is not always possible. My own museum decided to move ahead without all the recommended core documents. In fact, of the five core documents, we only had a finalized mission statement, a 10-year-old strategic plan, and a collections policy that was in the process of being developed. Why didn't we start with a new strategic plan? Our executive director was planning his retirement and wished to defer the strategic plan to the new leadership. Knowing how long that process would take, improving the visitor experience through an interpretative master plan seemed the best move forward for our site. I worked with our retiring executive director to write a grant that would provide us with the opportunity to generate the necessary discussion via an interpretive master planning process.

Other documents that will be used during the planning process include annual reports, site maps, interpretive manuals, a sampling of exhibit images, a list of 10 to 15 of the most significant items in the permanent collection, a list of public and school programs offered, publications of note, any recent (within last two or three years) survey results, and a list of key partners and stakeholders you wish to include in the planning process.

BUILDING SUPPORT FOR PLANNING

An essential part of any strategic planning is the support of your stakeholders. Board, staff, and volunteers all need to buy in, or any plan will be quietly put on a shelf. This starts with the executive director because without leader buy-in, no project gets off the ground. I started by working on an interpretive manual. We didn't have established themes for our museum, so I substituted state education content standards. Next, I conducted a program survey of members and staff. This provided some direction regarding what current audiences wanted to see but, again, lacked the consensus building that a formal interpretive planning process includes. The survey also did not solicit the board's support of whatever plan I came up with. Finally, it did not include important stakeholders in the process. While I was able to make educated guesses with my interpretive manual, they were still guesses. I communicated my concerns to our executive director, building the case for the positive impact an interpretive master plan could have.

After receiving the grant and, with it, the support of the Colorado State Historical Society, I wrote an article for the museum's in-house magazine, *Iron Horse News*, discussing the merits of an interpretive master plan and explaining how it would be accomplished. This conveyed to our audiences the actions we were undertaking. Finally, I made time to personally speak with my coworkers, reassuring them that their voices would be included in the process and that this would, in fact, enhance their work.

FINDING FUNDING

Whether you have decided to undertake the interpretive planning process on your own or hire a consultant, there are costs connected to these plans. Your budget should consider costs associated with staff time, consultants for writing the funding grant and facilitating the project, travel, meals and snacks for stakeholders, printing, office supplies, media (telephone and social media), marketing, and piloting programs.[5] Once you have a budget, you can look for likely revenue sources. You are probably familiar with a number of foundations, corporations, and government agencies that can be helpful. Some places to begin your search include your board, Google, local organizations for grant makers, regional foundation directories, the Foundation Center Online, the Catalog of Federal Domestic Assistance, and Grants.gov.[6]

Federal agencies such as the Institute for Museum and Library Services (IMLS) and the National Endowment for the Humanities (NEH) provide grants for interpretive planning, as do many state agencies. The NEH offers

Public Humanities Project grants that specifically support long-term interpretive programs for historic sites, houses, neighborhoods, and regions. IMLS has funded interpretive planning through its grants, one of the more popular being the Museums for America grants. There are also a number of private foundations that see the value of institutional/program planning. Examples of regional/state organizations that offer funding are the Colorado State Historic Fund, the Pew Center for Arts and Heritage (Philadelphia area), the Templeton Foundation, and the Andrew W. Mellon Foundation.

One of the best tools the museum profession has in place for evaluating where you are in your institution's development is the Museum Assessment Program (MAP). Funded by IMLS, MAP surveys work with small and mid-sized museums to reinforce operations, plan for the future, and address standards.[7]

There are five assessments available: Organizational, Collections Stewardship, Education and Interpretation, Community and Audience Engagement, and Board Leadership. Each assessment type provides participants with self-study workbooks and activities, peer mentoring through a site visit, and a report filled with reviewer recommendations. As this book is being written, IMLS is introducing two new assessment categories: Education and Interpretation and Board Leadership.[8] The Community and Audience Engagement and the Education and Interpretation assessments will be of particular interest for those pursuing interpretive planning.

According to the American Alliance of Museums website, the MAP experience works toward greater alignment of activities, mission, and resources by providing: an analysis of its strengths, weaknesses, and opportunities; a prioritized roadmap for improving operations and meeting standards; practices benchmarked to standards; enhanced credibility with potential funders and donors; improved communications between staff, board, and other constituents; expert advice, recommendations, and resources; increased capacity for strategic planning; and finally, preparation for core document verification, accreditation, or reaccreditation.[9] All museums can definitely benefit from the MAP experience using this self-study as one of the underlying resources for creating their own interpretive master plan.

When I was looking for funding for my project, I looked at interpretive master plans that had been published online for information on their funding. Requests for proposals (RFPs) published online may also list their funding sources. Your development staff may know of a volunteer or member in your organization who values planning enough to fund your project.

I wrote a state grant that fell under the historic preservation wing of my state's historical society. This meant that our organization must emphasize the importance of historic preservation in our interpretive master plan. Luckily, that is in keeping with the work we do. Other foundations and sponsors may have similar requirements. Be sure they are compatible with your mission statement before you take the time to apply for funds you won't be able to receive or use.

A good plan requires planning. First, after realizing the need for this new interpretive plan, you must identify the primary goals you wish to address through it. Then review core planning documents to make sure you are starting in the right place for your institution. Next, build support for the planning process among your stakeholders, starting with senior leadership. Lastly, find the funding to support the planning process. Once you have successfully navigated these steps, you are ready to create an interpretive master plan.

NOTES

1. American Association of Museums, *National Standards and Best Practices for U.S. Museums* (Washington, DC: AAM, 2008), 36–37.

2. Freeman Tilden, *Interpreting Our Heritage*, third ed. (Chapel Hill: University of North Carolina Press, 1987), 9.

3. Elizabeth J. Nosek, State Historic Fund Education Grant, Colorado Railroad Museum Interpretive Master Plan—Education, 2018.

4. American Association of Museums, *National Standards and Best Practices for U.S. Museums*, 59.

5. See Stephen G. Hague and Laura C. Keim, "Budgets and Funding Interpretive Planning," *Small Museum Toolkit* (blog), December 19, 2012, http://smallmuseum toolkit.blogspot.com/2012/.

6. Joe Garecht, "6 Places to Find Grants for Your Non-Profit," The Fundraising Authority, accessed October 1, 2020, http://www.thefundraisingauthority.com/grants /find-grants-nonprofit/.

7. American Alliance of Museums, "Museum Assessment Program," AAM Accreditation and Excellence Programs, accessed September 19, 2019, https://www .aam-us.org/programs/accreditation-excellence-programs/museum-assessment -program-map/.

8. Institute of Museum and Library Services, "IMLS Funds New and Improved Assessment Program for Small, Mid-Sized Museums," March 28, 2019, https://www .imls.gov/news/imls-funds-new-and-improved-assessment-program-small-mid -sized-museums.

9. American Alliance of Museums, "Museum Assessment Program."

Chapter Three

Self-Study/Research

When I worked in Honolulu, Hawai'i, the Mission Houses Museum collaborated with the Outrigger Hotel in Waikiki. The hotel paid the museum to provide a variety of historical exhibits for the hotel. Hotel guests benefitted from the cultural perk, and the museum received free publicity for their programming in Waikiki. Through that process, I met one of my favorite mentors, who introduced me to her version of the 80/20 rule. She certainly didn't call it that, nor did my mentor refer to it as the Pareto principle. Instead, she told me that she found that her most successful projects were 80 percent planned and organized before she introduced them to her team. Eighty percent meant that she had defined her vision for the project to customers and had the answers for questions she knew would be asked. I have found her analysis to be true. Whether an exhibit, school program, or the overall interpretive master plan, doing your homework always pays off.

This chapter on self-study is about that 80 percent of the work needed to create a successful outcome for the interpretive master planning process. A self-study reviews three basic elements of a museum: institutional knowledge, current demographics, and the visitor experience. It looks at the museum's history, its governing documents and policies, as well as the institution's programming. It collects an organization's specific demographics and those of its surrounding community. Finally, it uses surveys and observations to consider the visitors' actual experiences.

Together, the analysis of these components allows a museum to review how well the desired outcomes stated in their governing documents compare with their visitors' actual experiences. Not only will an organization better understand its strengths and weaknesses as an organization, but it will be better equipped to determine if it actually needs or is ready for an interpretive master plan to address these strengths and weaknesses. It is the first major step of the actual interpretive planning process.

UNDERSTANDING INSTITUTIONAL INFORMATION

All organizations have a history. Sometimes it is just a few paragraphs on the website, or can be found in past museum grants. Other institutions have published entire books on their organization's story. Whether short or long, the organizational history provides a good perspective on how the museum began, what challenges it has faced and overcome, as well as remembering those who have played a critical role in making the organization what it is today. Meeting minutes provide insight into the roles and relationships that have developed over time and created more effective ways to achieve short- and long-term goals. Some institutions even keep archival files on their own history that might include such items as planning notes for special anniversary celebrations or fundraising campaigns. Not only does this information help keep an organization from repeating past mistakes, but also provides ideas and even content for programming that triggers innovation. It can also identify consistent barriers to institutional growth. Together, these stories provide invaluable material for the interpretive planning process.[1]

We mentioned the American Alliance of Museums's core documents pertaining to planning in chapter 1 (strategic institutional plan, disaster preparedness and emergency response plan, and a collections management policy). The other two—mission statement and institutional code of ethics—are equally important to a museum's success. In fact, of the five core documents, only one is absolutely essential to have on hand for interpretive planning to begin. It is the mission statement. Though a valid argument can be made for having a strategic institutional plan in place, the mission statement is the foundational document on which everything else is based. Simply defined, mission statements are a museum's statement of purpose. They not only distinguish the museum from other organizations; they identify the organization's core values and the full breadth of its activities. More specifically, in the museum world a mission statement "articulates the museum's understanding of its role and responsibility to the public, its collections, and reflects the environment in which it exists."[2] A good mission statement clearly defines the organization's customers and products, making it a guide not only for daily operations but the foundation for future decision making. Part of a mission statement's weight comes from its approval by its governing authority. An organization's unapproved mission statement is just a nice idea. Without that formal board approval, this document cannot truly represent the institution's purpose and mission, and should not be used as its mission statement.

In reviewing your museum's mission statement, you may wish to ask the following questions. Does it cover the scope of our museum's operations? How long can this statement endure? Does this statement reflect how we differ from other museums in our geographical area? How do we differ from other museums in our niche? Do our programs and activities support our understanding of the mission?

The Colorado Railroad Museum's mission statement, "To preserve and convey the rich history of railroading in the Rocky Mountain Region through acquisition, research, exhibition and education," sums up the museum's efforts nicely. At the same time, the mission statement provides room for growth and flexibility so that it can meet the challenges of the day.

A final foundational document that has not been mentioned to this point is the vision statement. A vision statement should be bold and daring. It should be inspiring. Most importantly, it needs to be achievable. Vision statements talk about aspirational goals to work toward, focusing on the change you want to see. Why are these goals important? Because if you don't know where you are going, you aren't likely to know if you get there. Vision statements are extremely helpful when doing any institutional planning such as an interpretive master plan, as they can act as a compass to keep you on course.

Besides core documents and histories, you will want to review both current and ongoing programming offered by your museum. Do you have an interpretation manual? Do you offer tours, stationed interpretation, formal scheduled tours? Are tours specifically themed, or does the docent giving the tour decide what will be discussed? Are there reenactments or regular demonstrations? What items in the gift shop remind visitors of these experiences or further their understanding of the museum? Are there opportunities for visitors to tour on their own using QR codes or other technology apps? What interpretive signage is used in wayfinding, exhibits, and on the website? Do you offer messaging apps such as Skype, Facebook, or Twitter? What about school, family, and adult programming? Do you offer bilingual interpretation? Do you have a popular lecture series? Do families enjoy a hands-on discovery room? What about special events? Are your programs consistent in their branding? What kind of training is available for volunteers? Are training materials provided? How are programs marketed to the public? How do your programs distinguish you from other area museums? Do your programs show the museum's understanding of its role and responsibilities to both visitors and collections? Do your programs relate to your mission statement?

Another place to explore as you gather information is the permanent collection and archive. What is the focus of your permanent collection and archive? Are there any items considered the "stars" of your collection? Perhaps your museum has a particular object or document that is revered by the board, volunteers, and the comunnity (figure 3.1)? Are collections used in your exhibits, or does your institution borrow heavily? Does your organization "hide" objects in safety deposit boxes for safekeeping, or does the public have access to them for scholarship and enjoyment? Are collections and archives available to the public on your website? How does the collection exemplify the mission statement? Does the collection influence programs or do programs influence the collection, or both?

Figure 3.1. The Ruggles Quilt is significant because it is one of two quilts made by Nancy Ruggles in 1820 from left over silk scraps of Hawai`i's first sewing bee on board the Brig Thaddeus. Photo courtesy of the Hawaiian Mission Houses Historic Site and Archives.

Another area to explore is the role of museum staff in interpretation. What questions are staff members answering? What information are they sharing with visitors? Are they dismissive of questions that are obvious? Do they oversimplify or overcomplicate? How staff affects the visitor experience also affects the museum's interpretation, and needs to be examined.

The last three paragraphs were basically made up of questions. While some of these questions may not seem related to your interpretation, anything affecting the visitor experience by definition affects the success of your site's interpretation. Planning successful interpretation means being able to relate your institution's history to your mission, and your programs to your staff and visitor experiences.

While reviewing this information, spend some time considering how the different areas of your museum interrelate. None stand alone. Just as your collection helps define and inform what interpretive programming you offer, so your interpretative programming helps decide what objects are appropriate to add to your permanent collection. Both interpretation and collections determine what is carried in your gift shop. A museum interpreting the importance of the railroad's impact on settlement in Colorado isn't likely to collect teddy bears. Nor is Colonial Williamsburg, which is known for its interpretation of the American Revolution, the best place to find a Tinkerbell Barbie doll. The point here is that every part of the institution affects the visitor experience, and so every area needs to be reviewed with its contribution to the museum's interpretation in mind. Examining how the different areas of your organization interrelate and where that can become even stronger is worth reviewing as you begin the interpretive planning process.

Basically, it comes down to this: by studying our organization's history as well as the manner in which we choose to teach, discuss, and represent it, we are better able to understand how these shape our museum's community.

UNDERSTANDING YOUR CURRENT DEMOGRAPHICS

Demographics look at population factors such as age, race, and sex; and socioeconomic factors such as employment, education, income, marriage rates, and more.[3] Demographic information is critical in helping an institution define its current and potential audience(s) which, in turn, helps to identify visitors' needs and gaps in services.

There are innumerable sources to be found on the internet when looking for this information as it pertains to your community. The website Grantspace (now Candid Learning, learning.candid.org/) recommends the U.S. Census Bureau's portal, American FactFinder. It also suggests checking your local, county, and state government websites, as well as public and academic libraries for localized data interpretation. The Pew Research Center also has data sets. Another website, New Think Tank (newthinktank.com) recommends additional websites including City-Data.com, maps.Google.com, and censtats. Census.gov, among others.[4]

UNDERSTANDING YOUR VISITOR EXPERIENCE

It is also important to look at how some of the basic visitor needs at your site are being met. How do visitors find you? Is your website being updated? Is highway signage well placed? Are entrances obvious and easily accessible? Is the museum visually attractive? What about parking? Is the site well maintained? Where are visitors bottlenecking as they move from place to place within your museum? Are there safe and identifiable paths for guests to follow? Are there accessible and modern bathrooms? Are there enough bathrooms in the right locations for visitor flow throughout your site? Will visitors be able to purchase a souvenir or gift to remember or share their experience? If not, how are you trying to address this? Taking photographs to illustrate the strengths and weaknesses of your site will help you review these issues during the planning process.

In the era of experience design, everyone wants an opinion. In a single day, I have been asked to complete surveys for Starbucks, Target, AT&T, and Comcast, all asking what I thought of my "experience" with their company and product. The Disney Company is especially good at soliciting this type of information from its amusement park guests. In the early 2000s I attended Disney University's Guest Services course at Walt Disney World. Our instructor discussed how the company had hung different colors of ribbon throughout the property. Disney asked guests in exit surveys what color ribbons they had seen hanging from trees during their visit. The colors most noticed became the colors used for marketing the park. Disney recognized early on that we were entering a new age focusing on the guest experience and that this "experience" would impact every choice the company made. It not only accepted the trend but embraced it, making it an integral part of the Disney business model. Seeking customer input is now an expected course of action in business, and decisions are not made without that all-important visitor feedback tool—the survey.

It is likely that your institution has been collecting information from your visitors for years. Your cash register or visitors' log may collect zip codes, telling you what region people are visiting from. You may survey program participants for their views on specific programs, be they school tours, general visits, special events, or lectures and symposiums. You may have done your own museum-wide survey. All of these can provide important insight into your interpretive planning process.

If you haven't done a recent survey, consider investing some time in gathering visitor feedback on your current set of programs. This will be immensely helpful to an interpretive planning process. A word of warning, though—this is an area where directors, curators, educators, marketing directors, visitor services staff, and consultants can all be a bit proprietary. Staff members may feel that the information gathered by the survey is only good if they have coordinated it. Each discipline will have specific questions to ask. but generally, a basic exit survey looking at visitor experiences is worth everyone's time. Frankly, all feedback is useful, and there are a number of useful tools available to anyone wishing to develop visitor surveys.

Here are a few tips on survey writing that I have learned over the years from various professional workshops, classes, and knowledgeable colleagues:

- *How many questions*: The general rule is five to eight questions, but no more than ten. People are giving you their time, and this deserves respect.
- *How to ask your question*: Words are important. Instead of asking, "What did you dislike about your visit?" try, "How can we make your visit even better?" Both are looking for the same information, but by framing the question in a positive manner, the second question encourages more constructive feedback.
- *The order of your questions makes a difference*: I like to start with more general questions and always end with, "Is there anything else you would like to share?"
- *Remember your colleagues*: As the education curator, I am most interested in the "What did you learn/like best?" and "How can we do even better?" questions, but make it a point to ask, "Where did you learn about our museum?" and "What other museums/cultural organizations do you visit?" for the marketing director.

It is worth noting that there are likely organizations in your area who work together to conduct surveys that can provide useful information to your institution. In 2010, the Audience Insights Department of the Denver Museum of Nature and Science in Colorado decided to test a theory: Would museum evaluations and visitor studies be more effective if they were conducted jointly rather than as separate institutional projects? In 2012, the department applied for an Institute of Museum and Library Services (IMLS) 21st Century Professionals grant. The grant provided training on evaluation procedures for the 15 participating Denver metro area institutions. The resulting evaluation projects have helped members make informed decisions, and engage and align with their communities.[5] This group has continued past the completion of their grant, offering more training on evaluation and working together on pan-surveys that continue to provide valuable information on what regional museum-goers are thinking.

Another organization in the Denver metro area is the Scientific and Cultural Facilities District (SCFD). SCFD is a seven-county tax district that not only provides invaluable funding to nearly 300 organizations across the front range corridor, but as part of its collaboration also collects data from its members on an annual basis. This data provides invaluable information that helps guide organizational growth.

Self-study and research are critical in planning, as no two organizations are at the same place in their development. Some are defining themselves and writing their first mission statement. Others have their core documents in place, but see a need to update these to reflect their continuing growth as an organization. This is good and natural. Thinking critically about the information discussed in this section reflects your organization's journey and offers you the opportunity to see just where your organization falls in its development. Wherever you may find yourself on this spectrum is not a value judgment of your organization. Rather, by doing your homework, your 80 percent always pays off. It is important to show the relationships between the institution's information (history, core documents, programming, and collections), your current demographics, and your visitors' experiences.

NOTES

1. "Institutional Histories," BetterEvaluation, 2011, https://www.betterevaluation .org/en/plan/approach/institutional_histories.

2. American Alliance of Museums, "Mission Statement," AAM Ethics, Standards, and Professional Practices, accessed October 15, 2019, https://www.aam-us.org /programs/ethics-standards-and-professional-practices/mission-statement/.

3. "Demographics," Investopedia, September 29, 2019, https://www.investopedia .com/terms/d/demographics.asp.

4. Derek Banas, "How to Find Demographics," New Think Tank, August 30, 2010, https://www.newthinktank.com/2010/08/how-to-find-demographics/.

5. "About the Denver Evaluation Network," Denver Evaluation Network, accessed October 28, 2019, http://www.denverevaluationnetwork.org/about.html.

Chapter Four

Creating Your Team

The best plans are a co-creation of different participants. No two museums have exactly the same budget, objectives, resources or staff and so, there is no formula for who to bring to the table.

—Larissa Hansen Hallgren[1]

Museum planner Larissa Hansen Hallgren, is right: There is no one formula for who to bring to the table when creating an interpretive master plan. As she says, each organization is unique. There is an expectation throughout the profession that the final plan will incorporate a variety of viewpoints. This is, after all, the underlying strength of any type of strategic planning.

This collaborative approach has been the focus of articles, blogs, interviews, and books for the past 40 years. Both consultants and staff consistently propose bringing together a wide variety of viewpoints. In fact, as early as 1982, the National Park Service's *Interpretive Planning Handbook* was based on "the philosophy that broad-based groups representing a variety of perspectives and view points can best develop imaginative, but realistic, interpretive solutions."[2] This call for a variety of perspectives has not changed. If anything, it has become more important over time, and is now at the very heart of any interpretive master plan.

In fact, more and more museums want to follow the experience design models made famous by Starbucks and Disney. These companies provided guests with deeper, more meaningful experiences. One example of how Starbucks makes its store experience personal at a very basic level is by using your name. They even write it on your cup so that your name is visually connected with their brand. Disney's ability to get its guests to really engage with their experience is at the core of the company's success. The focus is on creating happiness. In fact, staff are taught that happiness is the company's main product. So now museum professionals also see the need to find processes that not only connect with their museum audiences, but help provide those "aha" moments that illustrate their organization's relevance. Sparking the visitor's imagination is no longer the nice and innovative thing to do but has become essential for our institutions' very survival. Working with people who come to the table with a range of perspectives provides us the best opportunity to do this.

There may be no one definitive formula for creating an interpretive planning team, but there are a number of resources available for helping to define the team that best suits your organization. The National Park Service, the California State Parks System, the Chesapeake Bay Office of the National Park Service, and the National Association of Interpretation are just a few institutions offering a range of suggestions for seeking out people from many walks of life who represent varying opinions and differing approaches.

Still, the old saying about too many cooks spoiling the broth applies. While you definitely need a range of input from your community and visitors, those thoughts and ideas need to be sifted through and organized for your interpretive plan to work. To do this, the traditional method has been to provide different forums for the larger, more diverse group to brainstorm their ideas. This is followed by a small group that deliberates over the first group's work, developing ideas into the themes and subthemes that become the heart of the interpretive master plan. Broad perspective and focus ensure a successful outcome. A coordinating team composed of three to five members who shepherd the interpretive master planning project through to completion and a second, diverse group of various stakeholders who provide the unique insight that inspires, supports, and strengthens the project are important. Both are given specific attention in this chapter using the Colorado Railroad Museum's experience as an example.

COORDINATING TEAM

Interpretive master planning projects are each unique. But no matter how you decide to organize and move forward with your project, there are some basic leadership roles that must be filled. These leaders form the coordinating team. Defined as project coordinator, project champion, and guide, this is the group that shepherds the plan through from start to finish.

Project Coordinator

At the Colorado Railroad Museum, the education and exhibits curator acted as the coordinator. The coordinator wrote the grant and acted as liaison with the granter, submitting regular reports to the granter. Next, the coordinator created a request for proposal (RFP) to hire a consultant, and established a process for selecting the firm that would act as the project's guide. The coordinator was also responsible for gathering stakeholder names for the focus group meetings and acting as their point of contact. The coordinator provided the consultant with the museum's core documents and other reference materials needed, worked with the rest of the team to ensure deadline dates were chosen and adhered to by both parties, and ensured vendors were paid. The coordinator also handled logistics such as food, meeting spaces, and office supplies like easel pads and markers. Last but not least, the coordinator checked in with the executive director to assure him that things were moving along as they should.

Project Champion

The executive director took on the role of champion for the Colorado Railroad Museum's interpretive master planning project. It is the champion who acts as the project's advocate, making sure that everyone is enthusiastic about the project's successful completion.

In this case, two directors were involved with developing the museum's interpretive master plan. The first brought a lifetime of experience working with the state's granting agencies, as well as numerous friendships with agency leaders. When speaking with these leaders, this champion was well positioned to explain our project and its importance to our institution's future growth, and ensure that it would receive due attention. The old saying, "It's not what you know, but who you know," exists for a reason. Because of his experience, he was able to use these connections to help shepherd the project successfully through the granting process.

When the first champion retired, the new executive director came on board and staff quickly realized that he understood the importance of interpretation. As the director, he had the authority to move the project through various hurdles. It was this director who worked to help not only our board, but longtime members, volunteers, and staff to understand what interpretation is and why it is so important to communicate a museum's message. This champion took on the public face of the project and fostered not only an understanding of the project, but also excitement about developing our interpretive master plan. Furthermore, he ensured that as the behind-the-scenes work was quietly being accomplished, the project was kept in front of our board and staff as a thriving endeavor.

While the executive director took on the role of champion at the Colorado Railroad Museum, this role can be assumed by a longtime and respected senior staff or board member. Whoever assumes this role must be able and willing to exert the necessary authority to move the project forward and engender board buy-in.

The Colorado Railroad Museum differentiated between the roles of project coordinator and champion. These two positions could be undertaken by one person, but each requires someone dedicated to your museum's visitor experience and the interpretive story being told.

Guide

Also known as a planner, consultant, specialist, or museum professional, the guide orchestrates the interpretive master planning process, facilitating the stakeholder meetings and doing the actual writing of the plan drafts for review. This guide can be someone in-house, or a specialist hired specifically for the project, or even a hybrid combination of the two. The Colorado Railroad Museum hired a professional planner to take on these tasks.

Choosing whether to go it on your own or to hire a guide depends on a number of factors—your institution's personality, the available budget, and you and your staff's available time are just a few of the considerations. Either choice has its pros and cons. Doing it on your own allows for much more autonomy, but also makes it easier to be sidelined by other projects. Worse, it can allow the project to be taken over by a board member or director with their own, more personal, agenda.

Hiring an outside consultant or guide provides an independent yet professional perspective. It helps keep the project on track and brings for consideration a new set of diverse experiences with other organizations to the table. A consultant can also draw out ideas and thoughts to which longtime staff may have, over time, become indifferent. However, consultants are also human, and it is important to be aware that they, too, can come with personal agendas. And they cost money.

Regardless of how your organization chooses to proceed, the goal is to decide whether an internal or external person can best communicate your organization's message. Fresh perspectives can be especially helpful. The best situation may be a scenario that draws on longtime staff's expertise and utilizes the outside perspective a consultant brings to the table.

In choosing your guide, it is important to remember that not all planners are the same. Interpretive master planners have varied backgrounds, training, and expectations.

If you decide to hire an outside consultant, you will need to create a request for proposal RFP. An RFP is a job description of sorts. Simply defined, it is a document announcing an organization's need to hire a contractor to supply a product or service. A good RFP should outline your project's scope, your organization's expectations for both the project and the consultant's work, and the format of the end product. There should be an application deadline given as well.

Applicants may have questions. Providing the project coordinator's phone number and email allows potential applicants to contact the museum for clarification. By posting questions and answers on your website, you create an equitable process by which all applicants have access to your answers. Not only does this make the playing field more impartial, but by providing more information, you strengthen all the applications for your project.

The resulting proposals should provide you with the background information of the company/consultant applying, a timeline and action plan for completing the project, and a quote for the cost of completing their proposal.

The Colorado Railroad Museum's RFP resulted in a number of applicants with varied backgrounds, including former Disney Imagineers, curators, exhibit companies, and acknowledged experts in interpretation. Part of my role as coordinator was to whittle down the field for the committee to review. My first cut took out those applicants whose proposals did not address our institution specifically. These proposals were obviously prepared as generic, one-size-fits-all documents and, for the most part, did not specifically respond to the needs listed in our RFP. Planners that made it to the committee for review addressed the goals of the project. Many of these applicants had contacted me with specific and thoughtful inquiries, which they then addressed in their proposal.

In the process of writing this book, I interviewed a number of interpretive planners. When asked what made a project attractive to them, I received a variety of responses, though all agreed that interpretive planning "is not a cookie-cutter process where one size fits all."[3] Every site has its own individual issues and variables that need to be addressed. The planners also agreed that good clients exhibited honesty and open-mindedness, were able to meet deadlines, were organized, engaged in the process, provided a specific contact person for them to work with, and paid bills in a timely manner.[4]

Planners also experienced concern about RFPs that did not clearly state an interpretive project's goals. This opened the door to the dreaded "scope creep," where the project changes after it starts. These potential clients were also seen as trolling for free advice on how to define their project.[5]

Museums should be able to answer the following questions before putting out an RFP: What do you want to accomplish? What change do you expect? What do you want visitors to do as a result of their visit with you? How does that serve your mission?[6]

Of course, people need to see your RFP in order to answer it. There are a number of places one can post this type of document. One of the most obvious is your museum's website. It's also a good idea to send it out as an email to your network. Our regional museum, and cultural and nonprofit associations were willing to put it on their job boards, as was the National Association for Interpretation (NAI). I also sent the RFP to interpretive planners. I knew some personally, but used NAI's list of certified planners found on their website. Other potential places to post your RFP include the RFP Bulletin at Philanthropy News Digest, and listserves such as Museum-L.

Government-owned museums may have their own requirements on how this process should be undertaken. Requirements might include posting on specific bid websites, rules on how questions may be asked and answered, and possibly specific timelines that need to be followed.

It is also important to note that the coordinating team may be joined by additional members at different points during the process. Scholars, surveyors, and educators, among others, are dedicated individuals who bring expertise in their fields, whether it is in subject knowledge, creativity, or influence. They will help prioritize and develop the ideas brought by the entire group, further ensuring the final plan's success by addressing both the community's and the organization's unique character.

STAKEHOLDERS

Just as important to the interpretive master planning process are the stakeholders. A stakeholder is defined as "one who is involved in or affected by a course of action."[7] When choosing who to invite to participate in your interpretive master plan focus groups, think about how to achieve the broadest variety of viewpoints. It is also important to ensure diversity. Board members need to participate. Their buy-in is essential. All staff should be included in this process: maintenance, education, marketing, exhibit design, development, membership, business office, guest services, and curatorial staff. Specialized museums might have specialized employees such as engineers, weavers, botanists, potters, cordwainers, or even language specialists who need to have a voice in this process. Volunteers working in all these departments should also be given an opportunity to participate. As an interpretive master plan impacts the institution at every level, it is vital to give those affected a voice. The plan is not only stronger for it, but its success depends upon it.

The Colorado Railroad Museum invited its business manager, collections curator and librarian, curator of education and exhibits, curator of rolling stock, education coordinator, IT manager, maintenance manager, special events manager, store manager, and volunteer coordinator to participate.

Staff is only one piece of the pie. You are looking for a variety of viewpoints, and that requires reaching out to your community. Longtime and new members representing various visitor types should be represented. Others to consider inviting include community businesses and nonprofits with whom your institution works. Fellow museum and related organization professionals, local government and community officials, and officers from funding groups and civic nonprofits are good candidates. Educators are especially important. Teachers who bring groups to your museum annually have great insight to offer.

Once you have selected your list, it is important to get everyone on board. Be sure to incorporate time to educate your team on just what interpretation is. During our planning process, we asked our guide (aka planner) to incorporate this into the group's meeting time. When our new director came on board, one of his first acts was to schedule two separate workshops focusing specifically on interpretation. He went over the basics, covering the work of Tilden and Hamm, then introduced the part interpretation plays in communicating the museum's message. Participants left enthused and inspired by a museum, their futures enriched with a strong interpretive message.

Working with stakeholders is a delicate dance. If the process takes too long, they can lose patience and you can lose them. If not enough time is allowed, stakeholders can become frustrated and confused, jumping to negative conclusions about the process and its success. You can lose them along with your project. It is important to communicate. This can be done through meetings, retreats, emails, and even institutional magazines discussing the project's progress. Having an open door with those participating in your plan is essential, as is keeping an ear open for any gossip that may need to be addressed.

At the same time, it is important to respect the fact that your stakeholders are people with lives outside of your project. Too many meetings can weaken your stakeholders' enthusiasm for the process. We are living in an era where people expect instant gratification. A project that can take one to two years to complete can be difficult to sustain. Laying out a timeline helps to keep things realistic. Another secret to keeping stakeholders happy is as old as time—feed them. Furnishing a quality lunch and delicious breaks show your appreciation and helps to keep up stakeholder energy. If you are able, providing other perks to your groups such as free tickets to an event or a special tour can help keep your team engaged.

The Colorado Railroad Museum's interpretive master planning process took about two years. While we communicated pretty well throughout the process, we hit a couple of snags along the way: a change in the museum's leadership, and the need to address a rather large elephant in the room. In the end, both of our snags ended up actually benefitting the project. As discussed earlier in the chapter, our champions each brought important traits to the project, thereby enhancing it. But what the museum did exceptionally well was to address the elephant in the room—our museum's stakeholders did not know what interpretation is. Once we realized this was an issue, the coordinating team hosted an additional series of meetings on the topic of museum interpretation and why it is important. This was followed by a second weekend workshop to revisit the issues we attempted to address in our first workshop at the beginning of the project. Though we paid to bring our guide out for a second time, the support we created for the interpretive master plan through this process more than made up for the additional cost and time. We sustained this support throughout the rest of the project through multiple emails updating our group on where we were in the process, and maintaining an open-door policy that allowed stakeholders the opportunity to ask questions. More importantly, 50 percent and 75 percent rough drafts were sent to stakeholders, inviting their feedback. The final rough draft was examined by a smaller team. This included the funder's representative, who had also seen and commented on the first two drafts.

There is no one formula for who should serve on your interpretive planning team. The coordinating team should have clearly identified responsibilities. Choosing the right guide for your museum requires thoughtful planning. Stakeholders need broad perspectives and focus, as both are necessary for this process. In the end, bringing together a group with a variety of talents, backgrounds, and points of view can only serve to strengthen a museum and its interpretation.

NOTES

1. Larissa Hansen Hallgren, "Interpretive Plans: The Spirit of a Museum," accessed December 10, 2019, https://larissahansenhallgren.com/interpretive-plans-the-spirit-of-a-museum/.

2. National Park Service, *Interpretive Planning Handbook* (Harpers Ferry Center, WV: U.S. Department of the Interior, 1982), 10, http://npshistory.com/publications/interpretation/interp-planning-handbook-1982.pdf.

3. Interview with Katie Boardman, Cherry Valley Group, October 17, 2019.

4. Based on multiple interviews with interpretive planners/independent museum professionals: Katie Boardman, Melanie Pierson, Rici Peterson, Jenny Rigby, and Lisa Brochu, August 21, 2019 to November 19, 2019.

5. See note 4.

6. Interview with Lisa Brochu, and Rici Peterson, November 17, 2019.

7. "Stakeholder," *Merriam-Webster Dictionary*, accessed November 25, 2019, https://www.merriam-webster.com/dictionary/stakeholder.

Chapter Five

Facilitating Focus Groups

Of all the things I've done, the most vital is coordinating those who work with me and aiming their efforts at a certain goal.

—Walt Disney

Facilitation is one of the necessary arts used in business for planning, developing teams, managing competing ideas, and achieving goals. The word facilitation means "to make easier, to help move forward."[1] Facilitation has evolved over time into its own unique field and profession. There are certification training courses, as well as numerous books and websites available to assist facilitators in their work. Basically, it all boils down to a facilitator's main goal, which is to keep the group on task and moving together in the same direction.[2]

Giovanni Ciarlo, in his blog *Gaia Education*, lists the following qualities of a good facilitator: values the principles of consensus, admits/corrects mistakes, is comfortable with conflict, is emotionally balanced, has a good memory, is able to synthesize, has a sense of humor, communicates well, is patient and flexible, has personal warmth, adopts a positive attitude, and has physical stamina.[3] Most importantly, though not included in his list, is impartiality. Almost every other website, book, or article on the subject maintains that a facilitator's ability to be neutral is essential. This means that though he or she may guide the group's discussion, a facilitator will not voice an opinion, sponsor agenda items, or have a stake in the discussion's outcome. While an institution can utilize one of its own staff as the facilitator or the interpretive master plan's planner, it can be difficult for staff members to impartially facilitate a major planning process. They may not hear others' opinions and ideas. Staff facilitators may be perceived to have strong opinions in favor of a particular course of action. If they think the outcome is already decided, stakeholders may not be willing to share differing viewpoints. Facilitators who come to the table with their own agenda break trust, and without the group's trust, the process is flawed and cannot be successful.

Here is an example of how being an outsider can benefit the planning process. When I worked in Maryland, my supervisor asked me to help facilitate an exhibit planning process for a naval air museum in Maryland. The board was primarily made up of retired officers. Board members came to this meet-

Figure 5.1. Melanie Pierson of Conservation by Design leads an interpretive planning workshop with stakeholders such as Jeff Taylor, curator of rolling stock at the Colorado Railroad Museum. Photo courtesy of author.

ing passionate about the project, with their own ideas on how the project should be structured. They proceeded to express those ideas under the impression that louder was better, and that it was okay to speak over or through whoever else might also be talking. Not one of those men realized they were being rude, or that their behavior was stopping the group from moving forward with the very project they obviously cared so deeply about.

After observing their behavior, I used a positive attitude and direct approach. Saying, "Gentlemen!" in a strong but courteous voice, I was able to gain their attention. One cheeky silver-haired participant said something about not being a gentleman. This gave me an opportunity to move the discussion forward, using humor: I informed them that my grandmother taught me that there was a gentleman in every man and that they were not going to make a liar out of her that day. Patiently, I continued by telling them that we would be employing civil discourse. This would begin immediately by taking turns to speak and by considering what each person had to say.

It worked. It was the right tone at the right time. The group was able to brainstorm, discuss, and prioritize the ideas they came up with—all because they had an outsider who was neutral and willing to set parameters that enabled discussion. Today, this group of men have completed a multimillion-dollar capital project that has transformed their small museum into one of the community's premiere attractions.

There are numerous factors involved in making a meeting or workshop go smoothly, including these components: participants, environment, agenda, time, and style. Consider the number of participants: Too many, and your meeting will need a number of small group sessions. The background and positions of group members, as well as how well they know the subject under discussion, also make a difference in how the meeting is organized.

Stakeholders can be invited to participate through a simply crafted email that lays out the project's purpose, the museum's expectations of them, the time it will take, and why they have been specifically selected to help with this important undertaking. Some stakeholders may need a personal invitation from the museum's champion or another member of the coordinating team who has a good relationship with the individual to bring them on board.

If for some reason you find that you do not have enough participants, widen your net. Ask those who are unable to attend to suggest others who might participate. Staff and board members can be required or at least strongly encouraged to attend by the executive director. Volunteers may also need encouragement. These people have been identified as stakeholders because they care about your institution's success. It stands to reason that they will want to help you achieve it.

Consider the timing of your project. Would it work better at a different time of year? Maybe Christmas or the end of the school year are not your best choices. To create a workable interpretive master plan, it is essential to have a variety of opinions and ideas representing all areas of your organization.

Next, ensure that you have enough tables and chairs, paper, pencils and pens, audiovisual equipment, fresh markers, and large pads of paper and easels for brainstorming. Arrange your tables and chairs so that participants can see each other. This creates a welcoming atmosphere that encourages discussion. Make sure people have access to paper and pencils. Place your easel(s), large paper pad(s) and markers at the front of the room where all can watch the group's thoughts being recorded. Check the room's temperature and lighting. Look to make sure window shades can be adjusted if you are meeting during the day. If you are meeting off-site, find out where the thermostat is and how to change it. Don't forget to confirm that appropriate refreshments are available.

Help establish the group's expectations by setting a manageable agenda that includes reviewing meeting objectives at the beginning, and go over the group's expectations for the meeting process in order to ensure everyone is on the same page. Planning sessions are often pretty intensive, so include "brain" breaks.

Plan enough time to complete the meeting's goal(s). Starting and ending on time shows participants that their time is respected. While it is tempting to wait those extra minutes for someone you know is coming, it will cost more time in the long run because the other participants will realize that they, too, can be late.

Be aware of the different learning and communicating styles in your group, and be ready to adjust the meeting accordingly. Attention spans vary, and a facilitator needs to be able to adjust according to group member needs. When energy lags or the room becomes too frenetic for thoughtful conversation, take a break. A good rule of thumb is to keep a presentation between 30 and 45 minutes. This allows for thoughtful discourse but isn't so long that people are unable to stay attentive. Another helpful idea is to change up your agenda. Include PowerPoint presentations that introduce concepts and review work to date, break into small focus groups that invite individual creativity, and consider doing icebreakers to help the group think outside of the box.

ICEBREAKERS

One of the facilitator's best tools is the icebreaker. Used at the beginning of the meeting, a successful icebreaker activity stimulates one's thinking, encourages ideas, and inspires new approaches.[4] In a word, icebreakers foster creativity and help ease participants into group discussions. There are literally hundreds of variations available.

One popular activity is the favorite character icebreaker. I participated in this icebreaker while attending the Guest Services course at Disney University located at Disney World in Orlando, Florida. When asked who our favorite Disney character was, there were numerous Mickeys and Goofys, some Alice in Wonderlands and a couple of Beautys and Beasts. Mine was Tinkerbell. She has been my favorite character since my first time at Disneyland when I was six years old. Since then, I have come to think of her as a kind of totem. The reasons I gave for choosing her at the workshop were that she goes after what she wants, she can make you fly, and she has the hips of a real woman. Tinkerbell has stood the test of time and remains my favorite character. As an icebreaker for a group gathered at Disney World to discuss how the park handled guest services, it helped set the tone for the following week beautifully.

The favorite character icebreaker can work for museums as well. Museums can ask their group to choose a favorite character connected to their site or timeframe or subject. They can substitute their favorite objects for the character. I have used this icebreaker successfully at living history museums, historic houses, and railroad museums. Another variation of the favorite character icebreaker is the favorites table. This activity requires participants to ask fellow group members to help fill in their table. It acts as an icebreaker that gets the group talking to each other.

Here are some additional ideas for icebreakers you might use with a museum group:

1. Play "remember that great museum" (aka "shared memory"). Have the members of your group find a partner and ask them to participate in a fictional "visit" to your museum. Working together, they "reminisce" about their visit by responding to everything their partner says with, "Yeah, and remember when . . ." Let the pairs reminisce for about two minutes and then call time. Ask pairs to share their last "memory." Compare the similarities and differences between the "memories." Ask the group how it felt to say, "yes, and" to everything. Point out how different everyone's story was.[5]
2. Start with a question such as, "What museum would you like to visit that doesn't exist?" Tell participants to "Let your mind wander, your curiosity lead you. Ask yourself questions like: What collections, exhibits, and programs would your museum have? Who would your biggest audience be?"
3. Play "object by any other name." Preselect five objects and place them on a table at the front of the room. Provide the group with paper and pencils.

Ask the group to think of a "funny" or "silly" name for one of the five objects. The name might come from the object's looks or an imagined sound it might make. It need not be related to the object's actual identity or use. Now, ask each participant to name their object and ask the group if they can identify which object on the table is being identified. Discuss why people made the choices they did, and point out the connections made in choosing the new names.[6]

4. Try a "company history" icebreaker. This works especially well with a group gathered for museum planning. Make a PowerPoint about your museum's history with a separate question for each page. See who can answer first. It helps employees learn more about the organization's history and builds an understanding of how the museum has developed over time. It also provides a great review for planning an organization's future. Here are some ideas for questions: mission statement, year founded, founder's name, first object donated to collection, the most important object in collection (this will vary from person to person), the museum's biggest goal, number of employees, the museum's biggest competitor (this may also vary from person to person), and current themes.[7]

Whatever the ice breaker you choose to use, make it relevant to the day's discussion. If planned well, icebreakers can provide insightful answers that will, in turn, help the group do its best work in planning the organization's story.

BRAINSTORMING

The central activity in a facilitated planning meeting is brainstorming. In *The Imagineering Workout: Exercises to Shape Your Creative Muscles*, M. K. Haley, technology resources manager for Image and Effects, defines brainstorming as "a process that incites creative solutions with riotous, swirling activity, thunderclaps of genius and sweeping winds of change."[8] Used widely since the 1950s, the concept of brainstorming was first introduced by Alex Osborn in his 1953 book, *Applied Imagination: Principles and Procedures of Creative Thinking*. While outside observers may see the process as creative chaos, brainstorming does have a structure. It applies the following simple rules: establish an end goal, there are no bad ideas, respect all input, feel empowered to build on the ideas shared, share the imperfect things, record every idea, be willing to be wrong, and set meeting time limits. Now a norm in the planning process, this simple activity helps an organization broaden its perspective in order to see possibilities it couldn't envision before. It is for the brainstorming exercises during your focus group meetings that you look for diversity when selecting stakeholders to participate in your interpretive planning process.

Participants involved in an interpretive planning exercise do a great deal of brainstorming. They spend time considering the interpretive master plan's objectives and goals that will move the museum forward. Group members explore the subjects they think their collections tell best, identify themes as well as the best methods through which they will interpret those themes. Along with survey results, the group considers which audiences their institution should focus on, as well as how to build them. Most importantly, the group or a smaller team uses this process to determine the interpretive themes that will consistently communicate the museum's message.

Like priming a pump to draw water, a brainstorming session works best when the group has been able to get settled through activities such as icebreakers or a theme-related presentation. Once everyone is on the same page, people are more open to working together and feel safer about sharing "crazy ideas" for the organization's future.

The traditional method of capturing those ideas is to write them down on the large pads of paper. A recorder is chosen to capture the group's ideas by writing them down neatly so that everyone can see them (figure 5.1). If it isn't possible to use the speaker's own words, verify with them that you have captured their meaning. It is important that everyone be able to see all the ideas generated throughout the session. Post the pages you have filled up around the room. Ideas spark more ideas, and if participants can't see what has been generated, they will be unable to build on them.

Once you have created a collection of ideas, hand out five, eight, or ten stickers to each member of the group and ask them to choose their favorites. Let them know that how they distribute those stickers among their favorite ideas is up to them. They can choose to use all their stickers on one absolutely fantastic idea or parse them out among a few ideas. It is totally up to them. Allow 10 to 15 minutes for groups to choose, and then step back and see the trends that appear. While the group takes a break, the facilitator makes a list of the top ten ideas for the group to winnow down to three to five upon their return. These are the goals and the objectives, audiences, and themes on which the institution's interpretive master plan will be based. They should be included into any meeting recap that is sent out to participants.

After the meeting, either the project's facilitator or coordinator should collect the pages. Numbering and dating each page will help make it easier to transcribe them into meeting notes later. When putting the meeting notes together, it is important that these pages are transcribed verbatim. Those attending need to see exactly what they saw at the meeting. No one has expanded their thought or changed a phrase. This is important for building trust in the process. Sending the meeting notes out for review further builds trust by showing another level of transparency. The transcribed notes are not only good for documenting a project's history, but also act as resources for future discussions.

A good facilitator can make or break the interpretive planning process. This person works to make the process transparent, act impartially, and draw people out so ideas flow freely. It is a tricky role, and those able to do it well can make the difference between an interpretive plan that moves the organization forward and a plan that sits collecting dust on a shelf.

NOTES

1. "Facilitation," *Cambridge Advanced Learner's Dictionary and Thesaurus* (Cambridge University Press, 2019), https://dictionary.cambridge.org/us/dictionary /english/facilitation.

2. Susan M. Heathfield, "What Facilitation Is and How It Is Useful to Employers," The Balance Careers, accessed June 25, 2019, https://www.thebalancecareers.com /what-is-facilitation-1918129.

3. Giovanni Ciarlo, "Group Facilitation—A Step-by-Step Guide," *Gaia Education* (blog), August 18, 2017, https://medium.com/@gaiaeducation/group-facilitation-a -step-by-step-guide-b55495b057aa.

4. Martin A. Sklar, "Yes, If," in *The Imagineering Workout by Disney Imagineers*, ed. Peggy Van Pelt (New York: Disney Editions, 2005), 9.

5. Dana Mitroff Silvers, "Using Improv Games to Foster Creativity and Collaboration," Design Thinking for Museums, January 27, 2014, https://designthinkingfor museums.net/tag/icebreakers/.

6. Alan Gartenhouse, *Minds in Motion: Using Museums to Expand Creative Thinking* (San Francisco: Caddo Gap Press, 1991), 43–44.

7. Ashley Bell, "Boost the Productivity of Your Meetings with These 26 Icebreaker Games," *Snacknation* (blog), May 9, 2019, https://www.snacknation.com/blog /boost-productivity-meetings-icebreakers-games/.

8. M. K. Haley, "What's Brainstorming All About?" in *The Imagineering Workout by Disney Imagineers*, ed. Peggy Van Pelt (New York: Disney Editions, 2005), 52.

Chapter Six

Defining Themes

I was fortunate to work at the Winterthur Museum, Garden and Library in Delaware between 2004 and 2008. The museum is the former home of Henry Francis du Pont and consists of 175 rooms and nearly 90,000 objects dating between 1640 and 1860. It is considered a mecca of American decorative arts.

The museum offers one-hour tours focusing on such themes as "Winterthur, Then and Now" or "Yuletide" (figure 6.1). Visitors can also request tours on specific collections like pewter, ceramics, furniture . . . this allows visitors to explore their chosen subject in-depth with a knowledgeable guide. During my time at Winterthur, the number one complaint heard from visitors was their frustration at not being able to "see it all" during their tour. As staff, we were allowed to take friends and family through the house and, inevitably, they too wanted to "see it all." I admit that I tried to be accommodating a few times. Each time my guests likened the experience to getting drunk, as 90,000 objects in an afternoon can be a bit overwhelming.

So how did Winterthur keep its visitors from feeling overwhelmed by the information shared during a visit? In a word—themes. Visitors choose between themed tours that focus on specific collections, the du Pont family, or a specific audience type such as families. No matter the tour's subject, the museum promised that, in the words of founder Henry F. du Pont, "The Museum will be a continuing source of inspiration and education for all time."[1] No matter which tour a visitor experienced, Winterthur strove to fulfill its overall goal of being a source of inspiration and education.

Figure 6.1.   Yuletide at Winterthur Museum, Gardens, and Library. Photo courtesy of author.

WHAT ARE THEMES?

One of the earliest uses of "theme" in interpretation was in William Lewis's book, *Interpreting for Park Visitors*, originally published in 1974. It is within the book's "Organization" section that Lewis discussed how to organize all the different parts of a tour in order to create a meaningful whole, stating, "One of the most important tools in interpretation is the theme."[2] William T. Alderson and Shirley Payne Low, authors of the 1976 book, *Interpretation of Historic Sites*, encouraged "a standard interpretation centered around . . . what ideas and concepts they (visitors) should understand as a result of their visit to the site."[3] The authors were saying that tours should be more than a "this is a butter churn and that is a chair" walkabout. Tilden's influence was coming to fruition—looking for ways to provoke and inspire had become the standard across the profession. Themed interpretive programming took the traditional tools used for organizing tours and upped the ante.

The word "theme" originates from the Latin *thema*, meaning subject or thesis.[4] Today, it is a word central to the work of any museum professional focusing on interpretation. Themes are integral to interpretive planning and, like a thesis statement, will provide a foundation on which to build all the museum's interpretive programming. Put simply, themes are relevant and concise thoughts that resonate with visitors.

Themes basically have three important jobs. The National Park Service encouraged the use of interpretive themes to link a tangible resource such as a historic site or district to its intangible meanings, organize interpretive products, and connect tangible resources to universally relevant concepts.

Universal concepts are experiences that can be found throughout human existence. They cross culture, geography, and time, and are therefore relevant to a wide range of audiences. Themes developed around universal concepts, such as hope, conflict, bravery, patriotism, or struggle, are meaningful to visitors who have experienced the same things in their own lives.

Themes are everywhere. Music, books, art, television shows, and movies are all developed around central themes. Each of these art forms is a type of storytelling that builds the story around a central theme. The word itself is powerful and has been interchanged with everything from an overarching idea to subject, motif, concept, message, or moral of the story. In the end, it all boils down to the same thing: a theme is the DNA of the story. It is the premise to be explored, and every choice an author makes will feed that theme if the story is a strong one.

An interpretive master plan traditionally establishes one overarching or main theme with up to four subthemes. While the main theme defines an organization's message, the subthemes support that overarching concept by approaching the main theme in a different manner.

It is almost impossible to discuss themes without briefly mentioning Walt Disney. While traditionally not appreciated by museum professionals, we do, in fact, owe a great deal to Walt Disney and the Disney Company, especially when it comes to the concept of theme development. In creating Disneyland in 1955, Walt Disney connected every element of his park to ensure the story he was trying to tell was cohesive: "architecture, landscape, characters, food, merchandise, costumes—what today we would call theming—all needed to blend harmoniously in order to further the story."[5] Disney used an overarching theme or story supported by a whole array of subthemes to create a new type of amusement park—the theme park.

Disneyland itself was influenced by early living history museums. Walt Disney sought inspiration from various places like fairs, farmers' markets, and museums for his theme park. He visited the Henry Ford Museum twice. During both visits, Disney engaged with themed historic experiences offered by the museum. With his family in 1943, he tried out a nineteenth-century bicycle along with his daughter. Disney's second visit was after attending the Chicago Railroad Fair in 1948 with animator Ward Kimball. The two posed for a tintype photograph at Greenfield Village, Henry Ford's living history museum.[6]

CRAFTING INTERPRETIVE THEMES

Crafting these themes is no simple task. In fact, you could say that all the previous chapters in this book have been in preparation for this chapter—focusing on theme development. To create the best overarching theme and supporting subthemes for your organization, you must first ensure that you have the following in place: a mission statement; a thorough understanding of your resources from collections and archives to staffing; and a good team of stakeholders. Each of these elements will help inform and guide you in developing the underlying message around which your museum's future programming will be built. Crafting engaging interpretive themes is the single most important piece of any interpretive master plan.

Up to this point, the main focus of this chapter is understanding what a theme is and what it is not. It might help to broaden that understanding to think of themes as having different weights. If we return to the analogy at the beginning of this book, themes are core concepts that provide support and, often, boundaries to an organization's mission statement. One might think of themes as the load-bearing walls that hold up the entire structure.

While theme development is something of an art, one way to approach this is to go back to high school. High school English teachers have developed a simple but effective formula they use in their classrooms for developing theme statements: topic + insight = theme.

The teachers ask students to list the topics they see in a particular piece of literature and use those topics to develop a theme. For instance, after reading a story, students are asked to list topics they saw depicted, such as love, pride, danger, trust, fear, peace, friendship, and perseverance.

In order to develop these individual words into themes, students are encouraged to complete a theme statement. This is done by filling in the blank after a sentence starter, such as "The author wants the reader to understand that _____." Students complete the statement with, for example, "The author wants the reader to understand that in order to achieve one's goals, one must persevere and face one's fears." The next step is to cross out the pre-written portion: "~~wants the reader to understand that~~ in order to achieve one's goals, one must persevere and face one's fears." Finally, the theme statement emerges as, "In order to achieve one's goals, one must persevere and face one's fears."[7]

This tried-and-true classroom method is one that can be transferred to your focus group's brainstorming sessions. Like the classroom model, begin by asking your focus group to list the important topics at your museum. Encourage them to use universal concepts as much as possible. Write each and every idea down using those infamous large pads of paper so that everyone can see. Try to group the topics in some sort of order as you go, as this will make the process go more smoothly later on.

The next step is to prioritize your list from most to least important. At our museum, stakeholders were given five stickers with which to vote on their favorite topics. Each person could use their stickers in any combination they wanted—one sticker each for five different topics, or all five stickers on the same one. Main topics quickly emerged as the group voted, and we were able to organize our potential topics from most to least important.

Once you have finished prioritizing your favorite topics, you use the top three or four to build engaging themes. Going back to our high school English class example, provide your focus group with a starter sentence or preamble, such as, "The Museum's message to the visitor is that . . ." If you think it will go more smoothly, do what our planner did—break your group into small teams. If your group is small enough, you might even consider letting the members work individually. Once they have developed an engaging sentence, ask them to remove the preamble. And voila. They have a theme.

Once again, the group will vote. This time the purpose is to rank the themes they just developed. More than likely, an overarching theme will emerge, and the group will be able to choose three to four subthemes from those remaining that best support this message. The remaining themes will fall under the subthemes for development into future programs. Your themes will still need some wordsmithing, but the essence will be there.

Your coordinating team or a small team chosen from the ranks of your stakeholders can take on the task of revising the overarching theme and subthemes. Take care to avoid using a passive voice. You want your theme to inspire people, not put them to sleep. Try using a "visual" language to create an emotional reaction. The final product will be an overarching theme statement and supporting subthemes that can guide your museum's future interpretive programming.

Good interpretive themes are complete thoughts—relevant, concise, provocative, and meaningful. What they are not: topics, titles, slogans, soundbites, headlines, questions, or commands. Most importantly, as you create your themes, remember that the ultimate goal is to provoke your audiences into thinking and developing their own points of view.

"The author of this chapter wants me to understand _____."

NOTES

1. "About Winterthur," Winterthur Museum, Garden and Library, accessed January 1, 2020, http://www.winterthur.org/visit/about-winterthur/.

2. William J. Lewis, *Interpreting for Park Visitors* (Philadelphia: Eastern National Park and Monuments Association, 1980), 37.

3. William T. Alderson and Shirley Payne Low, *Interpretation of Historic Sites* (Nashville, TN: American Association of State and Local History, 1982), 21.

4. "Theme," Online Etymology Dictionary, accessed December 30, 2019, https://www.etymonline.com/word/theme.

5. Donna R. Braden, *Spaces That Tell Stories: Recreating Historical Environments* (Lanham, MD: Rowman & Littlefield, 2019), 26.

6. "Digital Collections," the Henry Ford, accessed November 22, 2020, https://www.thehenryford.org/collections-and-research/digital-collections/artifact.

7. Laura Randazzo, "How to Teach Theme," English Teacher Help, Free Lecture Slides, High School Teacher (vlog), LauraRandazzo.com, October 7, 2017, https://www.youtube.com/watch?v=Hwbwdj4mAiU.

Chapter Seven

Putting It All Together—
Writing the Plan

Old Sturbridge Village is a living history museum that interprets the social and economic history of rural New England. Visitors are literally surrounded by the sights, sounds, and smells of a New England community in the 1830s (figure 7.1). In the late 1980s, when I was an interpreter at the village, each household and shop was staffed by two to four people. Each day, these interpreters demonstrated a variety of historic crafts and processes including hearth cooking for our visitors.

One of my favorite interpretive stories centers around hearth cooking at Old Sturbridge Village. It is a favorite because it illustrates how the careful planning and appropriate themes not only direct staff actions, but inspire visitor reactions. I was being taught how to cook on a hearth in the Bixby House. The menu for the day was a molded bread pudding. An older interpreter had been assigned as my mentor. As we went through the steps of making our pudding, we discussed with the visitors the tradition of more experienced cooks teaching younger ones. We explained that we were using the extra bread from that week's baking before it could go stale, and the butter was made earlier in the week with cream from the neighboring farm's cow. Visitors also heard how we might have traded with the tinsmith for the pudding pan, how the blacksmith repaired the kettle, and how we bartered with the storekeeper for ingredients such as currants, and so on, until we had incorporated, if not the whole village, a large portion of the community in our efforts for that day's meal. Using the process of making bread pudding, we taught our guests how interdependent our community was. In fact, in order to have lunch, we relied not just on our own labors but that of our neighbor and his cow, the village's tinsmith, blacksmith, and storekeeper. The bread pudding took a good part of the morning to prepare, and visitors came and went. It was only later, after I had unmolded a perfect pudding to applause, that I learned our visitors had left to visit the tinsmith and ask about making the mold for our pudding. The storekeeper and blacksmith also mentioned interesting conversations with visitors about the part they had played in my pudding. The fact that visitors were inspired to explore our discussion further by engaging with other interpreters throughout the village before returning to see (and applaud) the pudding being turned out was extremely rewarding to me. Good interpretation was more than just a good story. It involved in-depth interpretive planning and the execution of that plan.

Figure 7.1 Interpreter Ethan Choiniere discussing blacksmithing with visitor Julie Nosek at Old Sturbridge Village. Photo courtesy of author.

A PLAN IS A PLAN IS A PLAN . . .

So far, we have examined what an interpretive master plan is and why we need one: whether or not your museum is ready for one, what is involved in doing a self-study of your institution's resources, how to create and facilitate your team as they work to define the story your museum will tell, and defining the themes under which you will organize that story. This chapter looks at taking all the energy, thought, and work your organization has put into the interpretive planning process and getting it down on paper. It is time to actually write the interpretive master plan.

Easier said than done of course. The plan will be the written record of your work. It documents the research, brainstorming, and planning done by the museum and stakeholders. It records the decisions made and analyzes the factors that went into making those decisions. Finally, it provides a framework on which the staff will build interpretive programming.

To be successful, a museum's plan must be written down in an organized, prioritized, and—oh, we mustn't forget—inspiring format that all those stakeholders will recognize as the result of their input. If you are fortunate, you or someone on your staff or board can take the information you have gathered and put it into a written format that works for your museum. Or you have hired an interpretive planner skilled not only in facilitating all those brainstorming sessions with your stakeholders, but can also help you consolidate all that good information you gathered into a written report or plan. It is truly an art form of its own, capturing the ideas, decisions, strategies, and analyses of the planning process into a final document that will live on to act as a guide for the museum's future efforts. And there is no one right way to do this. Each museum is a reflection of its own very unique community, and what works for one will not work for others.

A number of interpretive planners have published their own books on the interpretive planning process. Lisa Brochu, author of *Interpretive Planning: The 5-M Model for Successful Planning Projects*, was the first to see the need to codify and recognize quality interpretive planning.[1] She led the effort responsible for the interpreter planner certification process that is still in use by the National Association of Interpretation (NAI) today. The 5-M model she developed has now been taught to hundreds of professionals through her interpretive planning workshops and is used as a textbook in many college curricula for heritage interpretation. Seen as a leading authority in the field of interpretive planning, Brochu remains a strong advocate for the individuality of the process, stating that "there is no template for interpretive planning, as every site has its own individual issues and variables."[2]

Arguably the most prolific author on the topic of interpretive planning, John Veverka also teaches the subject of interpretive planning through university classes, workshops, and internet courses. The process he developed with his team at HDC International is known as the Veverka Interpretive Process. It answers the "what, why, who, and how" for a site.[3]

Brochu and Veverka offer two models for interpretive planning, but as Jenny Rigby, principal at the Acorn Group, states, "It is not a one-stop shop. Planners can pull from multiple models to meet the needs of the client."[4] Government agencies such as the National Park Service, the U.S. Forest Service, the Bureau of Land Management, and the California State Parks System are among those providing resources for interpretive planning to organizations. Most of these government agencies provide a prescribed course to follow when developing an interpretive master plan. Yet even with the wealth of support telling their staff "how to" produce the desired interpretive result, these master plans vary within each agency. By their very nature, interpretive master plans not only reflect their institution's unique story, but just as importantly, reflect the individual needs and creativity of their communities.

At the end of the day, appreciating the uniqueness of every museum is more than just a little important. Your organization's unique character needs to be reflected in the written plan. Your final interpretive master planning document will be different from that of every other institution. Your plan will serve to relate, provoke, and inspire your organization's target audiences.

Just as there is no single model for developing an interpretive master plan, there is also no single way to write one. A review of numerous interpretive master plans will only demonstrate that no organization places emphasis in the same area(s). This is not only reflected in the table of contents, but shows up in the level of detail given in specific areas of the final written plan. Katie Boardman, a former professor of mine at the Cooperstown Graduate Program in Museum Studies and now a principal with the Cherry Valley Group, is fond of saying, "This is *not* a cookie-cutter process."[5] That said, there is general agreement on including these elements: defining the organization's resources; determining the target audience(s) to serve; defining interpretive themes, objectives, or desired outcomes; and describing methods for implementation.

If you do not hire a consultant to help with developing your interpretive master plan, then look at how others have chosen to organize their plans for inspiration. This will help you see how your professional peers have created the written framework for their plan. A survey of other interpretive master plans can also provide an understanding of current trends in the field, inspiration for what you want to incorporate into your own plan, as well as items that may work very well for that particular organization but definitely don't have a place in your own museum's plan. A plan's table of contents provides a potential outline for identifying, organizing, and streamlining the information you want to see in your own final written plan.

USEFUL FOR ALL

As you began the planning process, you likely encountered coworkers who brushed off the plan as not affecting them or their work. But assuming that an interpretive master plan will be used only by the organization's educators and tour guides couldn't be more wrong. As I noted earlier, interpretation is a team sport. One of the fundamental roles of any interpretive master planning process is building a consensus throughout the entire organization of what the museum's story is, from volunteer to curator and janitor to director. In fact, finding ways to build a consensus that will empower staff to move forward together as a team is one of the most often stated reasons for developing an interpretive master plan.[6]

Museums are known for the variety of disciplines they bring to the table. Curators, conservators, archivists, librarians, gift shop managers, educators, interpreters, media specialists, marketers, business managers, administrators, and development specialists all play a part in making museums the incredible places they are. However, each of these professionals also brings their own terminology, ethical standards, and expectations to bear. A museum is strengthened by acknowledging how each professional both informs and is informed by their colleagues. Nowhere is this better reflected than in the various strategic plans a museum develops. For example, the Ulster Museum, a participant in a European project titled *Teamwork for Preventive Conservation*, noted, "It proved helpful for staff to recognize that the problems they face are, more often than not, shared and are by no means unique to a particular staff grouping or discipline."[7]

The Colorado Railroad Museum's curator of collections, Stephanie Gilmore, stated it best:

> Essentially every part of the museum is affected by the Interpretive Master Plan, so it will play a part in every job within the museum. For me in Collections, I will use the interpretive master plan in my work to help guide both the Collection's policy and the Collection's plan. Knowing where the museum as a whole is headed will help guide my area's activities. Specifically, the themes from the interpretive master plan will guide collecting in the future, as we will want to collect items which directly reflect our major themes. The interpretive master plan will also help us with the deaccessioning of items that do not fit those themes or our scope of collections. Furthermore, the interpretive master plan will help us pursue grants as it is among the basic documents for museum activity.[8]

If we break down the museum into its main work areas (table 7.1), we can further examine how a museum's interpretation is intertwined with the work being done throughout the institution. In fact, to do its best work, a museum must present a unified effort that is aided by themes and objectives developed during the interpretive master planning process. Silos can actually endanger a museum's basic ability to carry out good work when staff work independently—or when staff try to make bread pudding independently.

Table 7.1.   Interpretive Master Plan Institutional Influence

Work Area	Inform the Plan	Are Informed by the Plan
Archives/ Library	• material in collection • collections policy	• collections policy • what to collect moving forward • what to deaccession moving forward
Collections	• items in collection • collections policy	• collections policy • what to collect moving forward • what to deaccession moving forward
Development	• what funding sources are available • existing audiences	• where to seek funding and make friends • audiences to pursue
Education	• existing programs that are favorites, revenue producing	• what audiences to emphasize when developing new programs • themes to focus on when developing new programming
Exhibits	• exhibit plan • facilities and resources available	• themes to focus on when determining new exhibit topics • audiences to focus on when creating exhibits
Executive Director	• all of the above and below	• all of the above and below
Grounds	• water sources available • amount of land available • animals and plant species sharing land with museum (chosen and volunteer)	• what safety features to install based on audiences chosen • landscape choices based on theming and audiences chosen
Guest Services	• share expertise and data on visitors • welcome and wayfinding process	• provide background information on target audiences, overview of themes
Housekeeping	• unique processes required by collections • safety issues	• processes to develop based on new audiences' needs and safety
IT	• available social media that works for museum • audiovisual media available	• utilize new target audience(s) and defined themes • where to place emphasis • how to develop social media (website, Facebook, blogs, podcasts, etc.)
Marketing	• marketing plan • review of existing marketing • identifying resources available within the community for "getting out the word"	• utilize new target audience(s) and interpretive themes to identify and define marketing strategy
Membership	• review of existing membership to determine support (use to identify stakeholders)	• Use target audience(s) and themes to identify how to develop membership that is supported by and will support the master plan
Retail	• review of current inventory looking at sales to help identify community's interests	• Use target audience(s) and themes to identify and develop store merchandise

Of course, the different museum work areas will have been involved throughout the focus group part of the process and, hopefully, that will be obvious in the resulting document. As this is probably the most challenging part of creating a plan that works, special care needs to be taken to ensure that the various departments in the museum are seen to be in alignment with the final written document. In a 1999 *Baltimore Sun* article, the Baltimore Museum of Art director, Doreen Bolger, said, "The roles of museums are expanding, and I think we recognize that different people have different contributions to make. It takes a lot of people with a lot of abilities and talents."[9]

A WORD ABOUT STYLE

There are some basic nuts-and-bolts items involved in the actual writing of an interpretive master plan. Remember, people actually need to be able to read it. Your document will need to be clear and concise. If you want the plan to be used, you will want it to make sense to readers both inside and outside of your institution. Using slang, or technical language, or formatting can make it difficult for your reader to understand just what you are trying to get across. On the other hand, incorporating any shared vocabulary developed during stakeholder meetings into the written document, and perhaps even providing a glossary of terms, lets stakeholders know they were heard.

A Sense of Place: An Interpretive Planning Handbook, originally produced in Scotland by the Tourism and Environmental Initiative in 1997, suggests resisting the use of museum jargon wherever possible. The handbook also recommends that the written plan should "avoid being too critical or confrontational: someone reading the final report will go straight to the bits that directly affect them, and may read these sections out of context."[10]

The Museum Galleries of Scotland website goes to the heart of writing the actual document. It recommends that before creating the written document, the writer should "know your space, know your subject, and know your objects. By employing an interpretive strategy which applies to the entirety of the exhibition or gallery, you will develop a uniformity of tone, delivery, and level of information, which is important as it keeps the interpretation focused which therefore focuses the visitor experience."[11]

As for any other official document, it is important to follow your organization's style guide. A style guide can help maintain a consistent approach throughout the entire work. It also helps you use quotations, cite your and other organizations' documents, and properly identify the information gathered through your multiple focus group sessions in a consistent manner. If your organization hasn't selected a specific style guide as a reference, three of the more popular are *The Chicago Manual of Style*, *The Elements of Style,* and *The Associated Press Style Guide*.

The final plan needs to be graphically attractive and easy to understand, utilizing tables, sidebars, and photographs to get its message across. Like any other publication, the final interpretive master plan should include a cover, title page, copyright page, acknowledgment of all stakeholders who assisted with the project, a table of contents, and an introduction. It should also include sections on resources, audiences, interpretive themes, objectives, and desired outcomes, as well as methods for implementing those desired outcomes.

REVIEWING TO ENSURE TRANSPARENCY

An essential piece of the whole process is sharing the plan's findings with your stakeholders and community. Not only is it immeasurably helpful to invite these audiences to read drafts before the document is finalized, but it can also keep the museum from appearing critical or adversarial.

Many planners begin putting parts of the written plan together shortly after the institutional self-study. It is also important to show transparency throughout the writing process. There may be a sense of a lot of time passing between the project's beginning and the brainstorming sessions, and that finalized plan. A good planner will more than likely choose to create review drafts that provide a series of touchpoints throughout the process. Usually, two or three drafts will do the job.

It can also seem like a long time between each draft of the project. You might send email updates of the plan's progress, or put short articles in the membership newsletter, magazine, or social media sites about the important role the interpretive master plan will play in the organization's future. These updates can go a long way in keeping the project front and center in stakeholders' minds.

It can be tempting to provide every draft to stakeholders for review. While this is sometimes warranted, it can cause the project to spin out of control. Don't let the main purpose behind doing an interpretive master plan get bogged down in details that aren't relevant. It is important to know, as the old saying goes, when to fish and when to cut bait.

Transparency is good. It makes the project stronger by making sure everyone's voice has been heard. It catches the important details that housekeeping, education, guest services, development, marketing, or collections deal with every day while the rest of the museum remains blissfully unaware. It ensures that by the time the final draft is put before the board, things have not only been reviewed multiple times, but there are no surprises requiring a major overhaul of the entire plan.

Consensus is vital to any type of master plan's success. While not every museum puts their plan before the board for approval, board support remains essential for the plan's eventual implementation. As you and your stakeholders review a written draft, consider whether the plan adheres to the organization's mission statement; addresses the goals the project identified at the beginning of the process; fully identifies the site's resources, audience(s), themes, and objectives; attracts the audience identified by the stakeholders with its newly minted themes and objectives; and reflects the input provided by the various people who participated in the process.

The "Executive Summary" of the Nova Scotia Museum's *Interpretive Master Plan* concluded with this statement:

> The Interpretive Master Plan is a tool for the Museum and the Heritage Division to utilize for many years to come. It is the rod with which to leverage funding, the flag to inspire museum staff, the handbook to develop interpretation, and the voice through which the Museum can speak to all Nova Scotians, reengaging them with their heritage in both new and familiar ways.[12]

As the end product, the written document not only records the decisions made and analyzes the factors that went into making those choices, it also puts it all together, creating a path for the museum to follow in order to achieve success.

NOTES

1. Interview with Lisa Brochu and Rici Peterson, November 17, 2019.

2. Ibid.

3. HDC International, "The Veverka Interpretation Planning Process," accessed November 9, 2020, https://www.heritagedestination.com/hdc-training---veverka -interpretation-planning-process/.

4. Interview with Jenny Rigby of the Acorn Group and Rici Petersen, November 19, 2019.

5. Interview with Katie Boardman of the Cherry Valley Group, October 17, 2019.

6. Leonor A. Colbert, "Practiced-Based Perspectives on the Interpretive Planning Process," (master's thesis, University of Washington, 2017), 29, https://digital.lib .washington.edu/researchworks/handle/1773/39766.

7. Neal Putt and Sarah Slade, *Teamwork for Preventive Conservation* (Rome: International Centre for the Study of Preservation and Restoration of Cultural Property [ICCROM], 2004), 1, https://www.iccrom.org/sites/default/files/ICCROM _01_Teamwork_en.pdf.

8. Interview with Stephanie Gilmore, February 27, 2020.

9. Holly Selby, "The Fine Art of Teamwork; Collaboration among Curators Is Aiding Many Museums. But Is It Aiding Art?" *Baltimore Sun*, December 12, 1999, https://www.baltimoresun.com/news/bs-xpm-1999-12-12-9912210366-story.html.

10. James Carter (ed.), *A Sense of Place: An Interpretive Planning Handbook* (Scottish Interpretation Network, 2001), https://portal.uni-freiburg.de/interpreteurope /service/publications/recommended-publications/carter_sense-of-place.pdf.

11. Museum Galleries Scotland, "Planning Your Interpretation," accessed February 15, 2020, https://www.museumsgalleriesscotland.org.uk/advice/collections/planning -your-interpretation/.

12. Nova Scotia Museum, "Executive Summary," *Interpretive Master Plan*, March 2009, xi, https://museum.novascotia.ca/sites/default/files/inline/images/executive -summary.pdf.

Chapter Eight

Creating a Plan for Implementation

It's not enough to be busy, so are the ants. The question is, what are we busy about?

—Henry David Thoreau

When the COVID-19 pandemic forced nonessential businesses (including museums) to shut down in Colorado, the Colorado Railroad Museum was no exception. Staff members were nervous, worried about what this would mean for their jobs, and a bit frustrated that all the hard work and planning that had gone into the multiple programs and special events for the upcoming spring and summer seasons would have to be scrapped or redesigned. Guests, volunteers, and staff were disappointed. Somehow, we needed to pivot quickly to find a way through this new reality.

At our last staff meetings before closing, we sat under our outdoor pavilion in order to properly social distance. We tried to figure out just how to carry out the state, county, and various city orders while still serving our visitors. We discussed the challenges of keeping everyone (visitors, volunteers, and staff) safe. We discussed how to close down those programs no longer possible to implement, and we worked together to determine opportunities the pandemic might open up for us. How could our museum stay on mission and make a difference for our community?

Soon my coworkers were coming up with multiple plans to present programming that had not been seriously considered in a pre-COVID-19 world where hands-on programs were the gold standard. We still wanted to provide memorable experiences for our visitors, but now these experiences also had to be socially distant, properly sanitized, and at reduced capacity.

We had been working on our interpretive master plan, and all staff had been involved in the process to one extent or another. The review of resources, audience research, and themes that we had created provided us with immeasurably helpful information. We were able to use this knowledge base as we reviewed current programming to see what could be translated into a digital format. Within this context we brainstormed ideas for new programming that aligned with the museum's mission and themes, as well as determined which programs on the upcoming calendar were no longer plausible.

A story and craft time was an easy choice for our new slate of digital programs. The existing weekly trivia question was also an easy fit. To these we added "Behind the Scenes," a look at the museum's roundhouse where we restored historic railcars for operation, and a bi-weekly presentation on different objects from our permanent collection and the historic railcars (figure 8.1). A new program, "Throwback Thursdays," provided an opportunity for volunteers and board members to participate in the new digital outreach efforts.

These programs met with great success, but would not have been as easily developed without the previous work we had done for the interpretive master plan. Our efforts have been appreciated not only by our members but visitors across the country, who are enjoying these new programs as well. In fact, the museum's social media traffic in 2020 was over six times as high as in 2019.

All of these new offerings were tied into the museum's new interpretive themes, reached out to our targeted audiences, and kept our message consistent. In turn, these new programs have strengthened the museum's overall efforts to make Colorado's railroad story relevant to our visitors online.

Even as a draft document, the interpretive master plan provided our institution with a structure allowing for both creativity and flexibility. It helped us move beyond the museum's mission statement by providing a framework in which we could adjust quickly to changing circumstances. While reacting to a pandemic was admittedly not in the plan, the work done by staff and stakeholders to put the museum's interpretive themes, goals, and vision on paper enabled the Colorado Railroad Museum to pivot when the institution's needs changed. Our plan helped us to continue to present a consistent story, utilize our resources more effectively, and serve our visitors during the COVID-19 pandemic.

A PLAN FOR THE PLAN

An interpretive master plan is a plan, and as is the case with any plan, it requires you to do your homework. This preplanning defines what you want to do, who you want to do it for, and the resources you have and need to do it.

Figure 8.1. Danielle Riebau, events manager, filming Stephanie Gilmore, curator of collections for Colorado Railroad Museum's Digital Program, "Small Wonders." Photo courtesy of author.

If you have done your homework, you have basically created a "to do" list for your institution. It is the doing of the to do list that we are turning our attention to here.

The literature on interpretive planning includes various approaches regarding how a plan can or should be implemented. Bureaucratic methods such as those developed by the National Park Service, the Bureau of Reclamation, and the California State Parks System might appear to be a bit rigid. At the same time, processes by professional planners and authors Marcella Wells, Lisa Brochu, and John Veverka allow for a bit more flexibility in a plan's implementation.

As implementing an interpretive master plan is one of the more critical parts of ensuring a plan's success, it is surprising how little space is dedicated to showing how to write an implementation plan, also known as an action plan. Most government agencies' interpretive planning guidelines and existing literature provide one to three paragraphs in total. In the National Park Service document, *Comprehensive Interpretive Planning*, the section on implementing an interpretive master plan is short enough to be quoted in full here:

Implementation Plan. This action plan lists those actions necessary to implement the Long-Range Interpretive Plan (LRIP), assigns responsibility, and sets
target dates. This section is a critical element; each Annual Implementation
Plan (AIP) over the next five to ten years will be based on this LRIP action
summary.[1]

While beautiful in its simplicity, this implementation plan uses a key
statement about tying the long-range interpretive plan to an annual implementation plan to ensure that the staff will carry out the plan. The long-range
interpretive plan defines the overall vision and long-term interpretive goals,
breaking them down into targeted, realistic strategies and actions. These actions are further broken down into yearly steps in the annual implementation
plan for the individual park to implement. This encourages parks and sites
to seek assistance for interpretive planning from a broader range of sources.
The intent of this process is to empower staff at the park level by giving them
more responsibility.[2]

The Bureau of Reclamation approach is more pragmatic. The Bureau
breaks the action plan down into the specific parts needed: resources, money,
staffing, effort, and timing/scheduling. Of those items, the most space is taken
up by effort and timing/scheduling. The effort necessary for completing the
plan includes such components as research, writing, graphic design, program
development, fabrication, and implementation. The Bureau recommends
incorporating standard workload charts, sequencing tables, or even calendar
software into the scheduling portion. A timeline is recommended for the design and development of deliverables, which should include content development (research and writing); graphic design and layout; and exhibit or media
design, development, and fabrication.[3] As these are the engineers who build
our dams, this level of planning comes rather naturally.

The Chesapeake Bay Office, part of the Northeast Region of the National
Park Service, developed *Interpretive Planning Tools for Heritage Areas,
Historic Trails and Gateways.* This document shows respect for an action
plan's ability to be flexible—at least flexible enough to address changing circumstances within a three- to five-year range. The region sees the action plan
just as much a tool for fundraising and a road map forward as the interpretive
master plan itself, and recommends the following stages: reviewing management goals, setting priorities, determining capacity, estimating costs, assign-
ing responsibility, creating a timeline, and creating an annual implementation
plan for a successful action plan.[4]

The California State Parks System also sees the action plan as its own
document; separate but still connected to the interpretive master plan. Like the
National Park Service and its Chesapeake Bay Office, the state knows that it is
easier to update an action plan by itself when there is a change in circumstances.

The book *Interpretive Planning for Museums: Integrating Visitor Perspectives in Decision Making* encourages staff to use interpretive master plans as "dynamic and useful tools" in guiding their interpretive program's growth. In fact, the authors list the plan as an implementation tool for guiding and contracting design development, fabrication, and implementation efforts.[5] They identify four other ways the interpretive master plan acts as a tool for an institution: decision making, development, monitoring, and marketing. Most importantly, the authors look at the implementation portion of an interpretive plan as providing the necessary guidelines to help a museum transition from planning to doing. This is done by providing more specific information about the budget, timing, materials, and effort needed to make the interpretive master plan a reality.[6]

Lisa Brochu included a whole chapter on implementation in her book, *Interpretive Planning: The 5-M Model for Successful Planning Projects*. She joins those who call for an action plan, recognizing that it moves an interpretive plan from dream to reality with defined steps for the design, development, fabrication (construction), operation, and evaluation of an interpretive plan's identified projects.[7]

A popular format for action plans is a matrix. The best matrices list your projects and include the following information: project title, a brief description, the responsible staff, associated costs, and a phase or year in which each project should be completed. By prioritizing your action items and including a cost for each task, you are better able to incorporate the plan's projects into your organization's institutional budget.[8] Invariably, surprises will come up that are beyond the scope of the immediate project. An action plan is a tool that needs to remain flexible and be updated as circumstances change.

There is general agreement that "taking action" is the key to success. The word "action" is defined by the *Cambridge Dictionary* as "the process of doing."[9] So it isn't surprising that government entities look to their annual work plan as the action plan for executing the interpretive master plan. More often than not, these work plans come in the form of a table or timeline, whether they are produced for a government entity or a private museum. On the whole, whatever form the action plan takes, it should include these key elements for each of the plan's top projects: timing, staffing, costs, resources, and evaluation.

Timing or phasing takes into consideration not only the order in which projects should be completed, but also the amount of time it will take to complete each particular project. Some plans can take between six months and three years, while National Park Service sites use their annual work plans to break down their comprehensive interpretive plan into doable segments as well as to coordinate interpretive projects with the needs of other departments.

In determining the order in which to do projects, keep in mind that some tasks may need to be completed before others can be started. There will also be work that can stand alone but needs to be done early on because of the impact it will have on your stakeholders' perspective on your interpretive plan's success. In its interpretive master plan, the Silos and Smokestacks National Heritage Area categorized its efforts as (1) Ongoing: projects currently underway; (2) Core: projects that need to be undertaken as soon as it helps to establish the plan; (3) Needed: projects that should be undertaken as soon as they broaden awareness of the area; and (4) Supplemental: projects that should be undertaken when resources and support are available.[10]

Activities will likely overlap in what will become almost an organic process that can be compared to a stone rolling downhill. Once different projects start being completed, others naturally follow, and things move more quickly.

The staffing segment of the action plan needs to consider the following questions: Which staff person has the skill sets to accomplish the different projects identified? Will a contractor or a consultant need to be hired? Can a volunteer(s) be utilized? Would a partnership with another organization best accomplish certain projects? How will staff availability/workload affect the implementation timeline?

Funding opportunities and priorities can and do change. Cost is perhaps the area of implementation that needs to retain the most flexibility. Projects need to define their own budgets for completion, and costs should be updated as needed.

Resources are the part of the action plan that identifies what assets already exist for accomplishing each goal and what needs to be acquired. This can be a variety of things including specialists, collection items, meeting space, staff, or cash.

Projects should have evaluation strategies built into each phase of the process. This review can take the form of a follow-up meeting or survey, and should include staff planning, the volunteers and staff executing the project or program, and visitors experiencing the program.

The final phase in creating an interpretive master plan is to create a method for implementing your plan. Most interpretive plans include a matrix for this purpose at the end of their document. It lists the top action items that arose out of the planning process and recommends the order in which each identified deliverable should be implemented.

While it seems like it should be easy to transition from devising an interpretive master plan to executing it in real time, it isn't. Care should be taken in developing an action plan. It is important to be both realistic and flexible in determining how to actually implement your plan.

How projects are described, where they are placed in your timeline, how and when they overlap, the money allotted to them, and of course how they will impact the day-to-day work at your museum all make a difference to your success. For instance, it is very easy to overload a part of your timeline, especially the first phase. Don't put everything in the first year. It is unrealistic unless you are able to hire additional staff to either handle current ongoing tasks or develop new programming so that permanent staff can change their focus. You will be setting yourself up for failure. Thoughtful, pragmatic, and creative approaches work best.

If you are working with a consultant, this is one place where their experience and background come into play. Someone with the actual day-to-day museum work experience will better understand the needs of organizations with objects and historic interpreters as well as their unique workloads, just as a consultant with experience in nature parks with visitor center exhibits and nature walks will have a better handle on a park ranger's workload. Any interpretive master plan will not happen in a vacuum, and daily tasks will need to continue or be revised to work with the new plan. This is a case where one size does not fit all, and a consultant well-versed in your type of institution can help things to go more smoothly.

In the end, it basically comes down to *who*: which staff is responsible for which project(s); *what*: the resources (money, facilities, materials) needed to carry out identified projects; and *when*: the sequence in which you will accomplish things.

Another key element is the amount of detail to include. As the old saying goes, the devil is in the details. Specifics can prove to be very helpful and certainly smooth the path from plan to implementation. However, caution should be exercised so that the amount of detail in any implementation plan does not stop your ability to be flexible. Balance is the key. Too much detail can be as bad as too little. Too much detail and you stifle creativity; too little detail and you cannot create a structure on which your plan can thrive. Ultimately, the action plan you develop should be flexible and something that can be modified to accommodate changing circumstances, experiences, and desired outcomes.

The who and what compose an interpretive master plan. The how and when define the strategies for carrying it out. A good interpretive master plan will prove to be an invaluable reference when incorporating an implementation plan that defines the staff, costs, resources, and evaluation methods to carry it out.

NOTES

1. National Park Service, *Comprehensive Interpretive Planning*, Fall 2000, 10, https://www.nps.gov/subjects/hfc/upload/cip-guideline.pdf.
2. Ibid., 4.

3. Marcella D. Wells, *Creating More Meaningful Visitor Experiences: Planning for Interpretation and Education*, (Denver: U.S. Department of the Interior, Bureau of Reclamation, 2009), 38–39, https://www.usbr.gov/recreation/publications/Interpretation-Education.pdf.

4. Chesapeake Bay Office, Northeast Region National Park Service, *Interpretive Planning Tools for Heritage Areas, Historic Trails and Gateways*, July 2010, https://www.nps.gov/subjects/heritageareas/upload/Interp-Planning-Toolkit-for-Heritage-Areas-Historic-Trails-and-Gateways-2.pdf.

5. Marcella Wells, Barbara Butler, and Judith Koke, *Interpretive Planning for Museums: Integrating Visitor Perspectives in Decision Making* (Walnut Creek, CA: West Coast Press, 2013), 44.

6. Ibid., 49.

7. Lisa Brochu, *Interpretive Planning: The 5-M Model for Successful Planning Projects* (Ft Collins, CO: National Association of Interpretation, 2014), 147.

8. The Boudreaux Group: John Veverka and Associates, *Clemson University Interpretive Plan*, March 2017, https://www.clemson.edu/about/history/taskforce/documents/Report-3-10-2017.pdf.

9. "Action," *Cambridge Dictionary*, accessed April 28, 2020, https://dictionary.cambridge.org/us/dictionary/english/action.

10. John Milner Associates, *Silos and Smokestacks National Heritage Area Interpretive Plan*, Spring 2003, https://www.silosandsmokestacks.org/wp-content/uploads/2013/07/InterpretivePlan_complete.pdf.

Appendix A

Introduction to the Case Studies

The five museums selected as case studies were chosen with care. I was interested in showing interpretive master planning in a variety of settings, so I looked for museums from various parts of the country—institutions that varied in staff size, type and number of collections, and amount of land in use. I also wanted to showcase the different methods used to connect with audiences. Most importantly, these case study museums took distinct approaches to creating a workable interpretive master plan for their institutions. The result was five sites that varied from a traditional historic house museum in Massachusetts to a historic railroad in Colorado and a palace in Hawai'i.

For some of the case study museums, the interpretive master planning process proved to be very successful. These museums used and continue to use their plans to guide future programming, help shape their collections, and reach out to new audiences. One institution found the self-study process very helpful, but realized that the resulting interpretive plan did not align with its institutional values. Its plan didn't make it to the proverbial shelf, but was thrown out.

A couple of our case studies employed professional planners to assist them in developing their plans. Others chose to undertake the process on their own. The resulting plans met the needs of each organization, helping them develop a consistent message relevant to their visitors in today's world.

Museums around the world differ from one another. Whether it is the collections they care for, the staff hired, exhibits presented, or the programming offered, no one museum can work exactly like another. I see this as a strength because it means as we forge our own paths, our colleagues provide myriad examples that we can use to support our efforts. As we explore the different methodologies these five museums used in pursuing an interpretive master plan, we can adapt the techniques that might work best for our own institutions while discarding those that are not a good fit.

It is my hope that the following case studies serve to underline the fact that there is truly no one "right" way to develop an interpretive master plan. But by exploring our strengths and pointing out where we can do even better, working with our stakeholders to envision what we want our museum to be, and creating a plan to get there . . . we can find a process that works well for our own institution.

Appendix B

The House of the Seven Gables

Founded: 1910
Location: Salem, Massachusetts
Mission Statement: To be a welcoming, thriving historic site and community resource that engages people of all backgrounds in our inclusive American story.
Target Audience:
- Tourists
- School groups
- Diverse visitors: immigrants, African American families

Themes: The legacy of maritime fortune coupled with Nathaniel Hawthorne's fame allows for the House of the Seven Gables to provide vital settlement services to Salem's immigrant community.
- Built by maritime fortunes
- Popularized by a great American novel
- Saved by service to Salem

Interpretive Master Plan Completed: April 2019

To the best of the museum's knowledge, the current interpretive master plan, produced in 2018, is the only interpretive master plan the institution has had. The plan was developed hand in hand with the site's strategic plan and is intended to set the stage for a richer interpretation of the museum.

It began innocently enough with the museum wanting to restore two rooms that would then be incorporated into their museum tour. Like many museums, the House of the Seven Gables submitted an application to the National Endowment for the Humanities (NEH) to fund the restoration and, like many museums, was refused funding. One reason cited for NEH's refusal was the lack of a campus-wide interpretive master plan, which provided the nudge the museum needed. The museum asked the National Trust for Preservation, which had previously awarded the grant for the original restoration project, if it could apply those awarded funds toward an interpretive master plan. With the National Trust's approval, the museum began work on the project that would transform the visitor experience at the House of the Seven Gables.

The House of the Seven Gables considers its signature program to be the traditional guided tour. The iconic site enjoys a robust tour program (up to 60 tours a day) welcoming 100,000 visitors annually. About 30 percent of those guests visit the historic site located in Salem, Massachusetts, during the month of October.

The interpretive master planning process provided an opportunity for staff/ volunteers to have a voice in the site's programming. They expressed concerns about having too many people on a tour, the need to be able to facilitate a tour that addressed their guests' interests, and a wish to move away from the scripted tour. Further conversations saw staff discussing the site's history, providing additional opportunities to include the story of enslaved people, migrants, and immigration stories.

What began as a restoration project grew into an interpretive master plan with the goals of building consensus on the museum's interpretive message; moving away from a generic interpretation toward a more deeply themed tour; and building consensus between volunteers, staff, and the museum board.

IMPLEMENTING THE INTERPRETIVE MASTER PLAN IN DAY-TO-DAY PROGRAMING

To ensure that its interpretive master plan is more than a shelf ornament, the museum has committed to an annual work plan that it hopes will allow the site to implement most recommendations in the interpretive plan in about a five-year span. The plan is also seen as a tool that will help Seven Gables secure funding for the projects it has identified such as creating a pre-visit signage program, developing signature theme tours, producing an introduction video, developing a school prep guide, and forming an interpretive committee.

The planning process provided staff with the much-needed opportunity to work through some of the challenges the site was being presented with daily. The House of the Seven Gables has always depended on guided tours. Whether or not this was the best approach for the site was evaluated, and a number of options were considered. The final determination was that the guided tour was indeed an essential part of the museum's offerings. Not only did the visitor want it, but it was necessary to manage museum logistics.

What the site evaluation did reveal was that staffing and timing were two challenges that needed to be addressed. The result was a more flexible rotation that took various levels of visitation into account. The museum sees this as a game-changer for how it schedules and works with interpretive staff, resulting in a more efficient program that provides ample downtime for breaks and rejuvenation.

Change is certainly NOT easy. There have been challenges at every staffing level and at each part of the planning and implementation process. With so many talented people, there is a wealth of ideas and visions—while a blessing, this is also a challenge. Consensus building takes a tremendous amount of time and is crucial for making grand changes to an organization's functionality.

While the project utilized many staff members' opinions, some staff spoke out more than others. It was not unusual to find quieter committee members having the most actionable path forward. In a room with a lot of personalities and visions, it was important to ensure that one or two people could not ramrod the process. It was and remains important to build consensus.

ADVICE TO OTHER ORGANIZATIONS UNDERTAKING AN INTERPRETIVE MASTER PLAN

Julie Arrison-Bishop, the museum's community engagement director, oversaw the project from the museum's end and shared what it was like to undertake an interpretive master planning process.[1] She emphasized the importance of using an open forum in any museum planning process, as the information gathered can set the stage for long-term change. All stakeholders need an opportunity to share what is on their mind. Consensus and repeating back information was also important to ensure that voices were heard.

Arrison-Bishop also found that working with consultants helped to keep meetings on track and that they were, in fact, an important part of defining the plan's final structure. The consultants entered the process as objective observers of the House of the Seven Gable's culture and logistics, and were able to provide valuable suggestions for change. Museum staff often joked and called them the "cool uncles" that you would listen to—because no one inherently wants to listen to their parents (i.e., the senior staff).

NOTE

1. Interview with Julie Arrison-Bishop, June 30, 2020.

Appendix C

Silos and Smokestacks National Heritage Area

Founded: Spring 2003

Location: The National Heritage Area is comprised of 37 counties in northeastern Iowa

Mission Statement: Silos and Smokestacks preserves and tells the story of American agriculture through partnerships and activities that celebrate the land, people, and communities of the area.

Target Audiences:
- Residents
- Repeat visitors
- Students
- Motorcoach tours
- Heritage travelers
- Families
- Niche travelers
- Recreation seekers
- International visitors
- Business travelers
- Through travelers
- Travel writers, guidebook editors, travel associations
- Distance "visitors"

Themes:
- The Fertile Land: Working the lands of northeast Iowa has fostered a connection between humans and the earth.
- Farmers and Families: Farm life and farming culture present images, at once nostalgic and ever-changing, of middle America and the values the nation espouses.

- The Changing Farm: The role of agriculture in American life and psychology has evolved as changes in farming techniques and technology transform the relationships between farmers, consumers, and the land.
- Higher Yields: The Science and Technology of Agriculture. Improvements in science and technology—employing the farmers' ethic of trying to receive the best return for their efforts—have yielded revolutionary expansions in productivity.
- From Farm to Factory: Agribusiness in Iowa. Farming and the processing of raw agricultural goods into finished products has grown from local networks serving local consumers to a multibillion-dollar industry, knitting together farmers, farmlands, markets, and consumers around the world.
- Organizing for Agriculture: Policies and Politics. In response to the changing roles of agriculture in American life, farmers have employed a great variety of strategies to protect and sustain their lifestyles and livelihoods.

Interpretive Master Plan Completed: Spring 2003

In 1984, President Ronald Reagan referred to National Heritage Areas as "a new kind of national park"[1] that married heritage conservation, recreation, and economic development. Today, the Silos and Smokestacks National Heritage Area (S&SNHA) in Iowa is one of 55 National Heritage Areas that work with communities to connect their unique heritage to local matters. S&SNHA is comprised of over 120 partner organizations that stretch over 37 counties in the northeast part of the state.

Affiliated with the National Park Service, National Heritage Areas are required to have a partnership management plan that calls out how the area's story will be structured and asks each area to demonstrate how they will operate.

Originally written in 2003, S&SNHA's interpretive master plan continues to be integral to the work done by the heritage area. An underlying goal of Silos and Smokestacks was "the creation of a cohesive interpretive experience across the region."[2] It does this by breaking down the story into six overarching themes that serve to help partner organizations align their interpretations with each other. These themes are: The Fertile Land; Farmers and Families; The Changing Farm; Higher Yields: The Science and Technology of Agriculture; From Farm to Factory: Agribusiness in Iowa; and Organizing for Agriculture: Policies and Politics.[3] Partner sites must identify their strengths in telling the six stories in their applications, demonstrating their ability to tell at least one theme well. The themes assist partner organizations in providing a more comprehensive message to guests while at the same time allowing enough flexibility to address a wide range of unique organizational missions.

In addition to providing a structure for the messages being conveyed to residents and visitors, the plan identifies audiences and advises partners on how to develop strategies for shaping their visitors' experience.[4]

IMPLEMENTING THE INTERPRETIVE MASTER PLAN IN DAY-TO-DAY PROGRAMMING

Silos and Smokestacks's director of partnerships, Candy Welch-Streed, shared that the plan is used daily in a variety of areas, including the initial application process, internships, outdoor signage projects, exhibits, and training.

Initially, the story can be overwhelming to partner organizations, but when they begin to see interpretation as storytelling and learn how to break it down into themes, it becomes more digestible. S&SNHA developed a workbook, *An Interpretation Manual for Silos and Smokestacks National Heritage Area* (available at www.silosandsmokestacks.org/partner/partner-resources/ssnha -interpretation-manual/) for group training that helps organizations new to interpretation make it more manageable. The workbook differs from a traditional museum's interpretive manual by providing step-by-step directions for creating an interpretive strategy for individual sites, complete with worksheets that will help them link their projects to the larger themes and missions of the National Heritage Area. It gives people permission to narrow down or focus their message, which in turn has made the experience more impactful. One specific program that used the workbook to its advantage was a signage project for a community college with a dairy center. Using S&SNHA's interpretive manual, the college was able to discuss natural conservation practices in an interpretive format that related to its readers and went beyond the traditional "textbook on a stick" approach. In fact, interpretation has moved beyond "Old McDonald Had a Farm" to more complex and challenging stories such as animal rights, global warming, and essential workers. In fact, during COVID-19, organizations found that going back to the themes helped them connect with their audiences and kept them going through a challenging time.

ADVICE TO OTHER ORGANIZATIONS UNDERTAKING AN INTERPRETIVE MASTER PLAN

When asked what advice she thought might be helpful to other museums, Welch-Streed reminded us that an interpretive master plan is just a framework to help guide us and won't always perfectly align with our efforts to increase the quality of the visitor experiences. There is always more to share, more stories to be told. The document an organization creates needs to be flexible so that it can grow and change along with its organizations. Secondly, she reminded us that it is essential to involve as many other perspectives as possible to arrive at the best possible end product. Finally, she recommended using the interpretive plan with your projects to help sustain the plan and its vision. In fact, she said, "We utilize our plan daily."[5]

NOTES

1. National Park Service, "National Heritage Areas: Community-Led Conservation and Development," last updated March 15, 2019, https://www.nps.gov/subjects/heritageareas/index.htm..

2. John Milner Associates, *Silos and Smokestacks National Heritage Area Interpretive Plan*, Spring 2003, iii, https://www.silosandsmokestacks.org/wp-content/uploads/2013/07/InterpretivePlan_complete.pdf.

3. Ibid, iii–iv.

4. Ibid, iv.

5. Interview with Candy Welch-Streed, August 12, 2020.

Appendix D

Cumbres and Toltec Scenic Railroad

Founded: 1970

Location: Chama, New Mexico

Mission Statement: The Commission's mission is to preserve and develop the Cumbres and Toltec Scenic Railroad, a historical nineteenth-century railroad "Museum on Wheels," for the education, enlightenment and enjoyment of future generations.[1]

Our mission is to preserve and interpret the railroad and to support its operation for the people of Colorado and New Mexico who own it, and the tens of thousands of visitors who come to be transported back in time through the beauty of the San Juan Mountains.[2]

Target Audience: Families

Themes: Not applicable

Interpretive Master Plan Completed: April 2010

The Cumbres and Toltec Scenic Railroad did not find their interpretive master plan helpful in the traditional sense. While their plan did not even make its way to the proverbial shelf, it did serve to reconfirm the organization's core value—authenticity. It also clarified how those responsible for the day-to-day running of the railroad saw their organization. The Cumbres and Toltec Scenic Railroad remains a short line railroad that transports passengers for 64 miles between Antonito, Colorado, and Chama, New Mexico, giving them an experience of the authentic West.[3]

In 2008, the Friends of the Cumbres and Toltec Scenic Railroad engaged a museum exhibit planning and design firm to conduct a visioning session for a proposed visitor center in Chama, New Mexico. The resulting vision statement recommended the organization complete an interpretive master plan.

The Friends hired the original consultants to also complete the recommended interpretive master plan.

The consultants created a plan that they believed laid the intellectual groundwork for expanding the story of the Cumbres and Toltec Scenic Railroad. The plan emphasized a proposed Railroad Visitor Center adjacent to the Chama, New Mexico, railyard and included suggestions for interpretive exhibits.

Early in the document, the authors were careful to cite the pride that the Cumbres and Toltec Scenic Railroad has in the authentic experience their visitors enjoy. Yet, they go on to recommend introducing multimedia, large invasive signage, as well as exhibit props and dioramas that would infringe upon the immersive experience so valued by the railroad and its customers.[4]

When John Bush was hired as the railroad's new president and general manager on January 1, 2012, he did not agree with this new interpretive master plan. Bush felt that the museum's original vision of providing people with the whole experience from soup to nuts still worked. As he put it, "We differed because we had the real stuff, so anything we added to it would subtract from the experience because we have the real stuff."[5] For his organization, he felt a lot of envisioning just seemed impractical and would be time better spent on keeping the historic locomotives and railcars in good working order.

Today the Cumbres and Toltec Scenic Railroad continues to transport people back to 1880. Anything that gets in the way of that experience in its totality is in the way.[6] Bush continues to feel that the new interpretive plan, while aspirational, detracted from the immersive experience the railroad prides itself on. For him, the final straw was the plan's recommendation to remove two original boilers from the boiler room in order to make room for a theater. "Destroying the real authentic thing to create a false space was not the direction the organization wanted to go."[7]

The plan is not used.

NOTES

1. Cumbres and Toltec Scenic Railroad Commission, "Mission Statement," accessed June 25, 2020, http://commission.ctsrr.com/about/.

2. Friends of the Cumbres and Toltec Scenic Railroad, "About Us," accessed June 25, 2020, https://www.cumbrestoltec.org/about-us/mission.html.

3. Cumbres and Toltec Scenic Railroad, "About Us," accessed June 25, 2020, https://cumbrestoltec.com/about-us-2/.

4. Andrew Merrill and Associates, *The Cumbres and Toltec Scenic Railroad Interpretive Master Plan*, April 2010.

5. Interview with John Bush, June 30, 2020.

6. Ibid.

7. Ibid.

Appendix E
Old Sturbridge Village

Founded: 1935, opened as Old Sturbridge Village June 8, 1946
Location: Sturbridge, Massachusetts
Mission Statement: Old Sturbridge Village, a museum and learning resource of New England life, invites each visitor to find meaning, pleasure, relevance, and inspiration through the exploration of history.
Target Audiences:
- History buffs
- Hands-on learners
- Guide groupies
- Family focusers

Themes: Foundations of interpretation create an impactful visitor experience, connect with a modern audience, and better reflects the diversity of our community both past and present.
- The role of agriculture and food in nineteenth-century rural New England
- The role of identity in nineteenth-century rural New England
- The role of public life and private life in nineteenth-century rural New England
- The role of trade and exchange in nineteenth-century rural New England

Interpretive Master Plan Completed: 2019

The decision to develop an interpretive master plan arrived somewhat organically, according to Caitlin Emery Avenia, the curatorial director at Old Sturbridge Village (OSV). In 2014, the museum underwent a shift in leadership within its Museum Program Division. Rather than reporting to a vice president, new leaders in education, interpretation, and collections now reported directly to the CEO. Acting in concert as OSV's program leadership team, this new team was specifically designed to focus on the museum's core.

The economic challenges over the last three decades had hurt the museum. Old Sturbridge Village had been forced to de-emphasize its celebrated costumed interpretation. It had also gutted the research, curatorial, and library departments. While the work done by these professionals remained, ongoing efforts were not what they had been. This made it unsurprising that some interpretive scenarios had not been significantly altered since the 1970s. If the team wanted to double down and return its focus to the famed costumed interpretation that had proved so successful in the past, it would need to rebuild its underlying structure incorporating current scholarship.

Another area the team wanted to build on was the museum's ability to tell an inclusive story of 1830s life, with equal emphasis on traditional trade shops, domestic skills, and trade. Old Sturbridge Village had been working on multicultural interpretation for decades, but wanted to take the opportunity to build on that commitment by broadening efforts to take into account not just race, but gender, class, and ethnic identities as well.

Seeing an opportunity to do even more, the program leadership team applied for a planning grant from the National Endowment for the Humanities (NEH) to support the development of a new interpretation and education plan. NEH funded this project at the highest level, $75,000. To complete the grant, the museum assembled a working group composed of the three department leaders, a longtime staff person with institutional knowledge, and a project manager who coordinated their efforts. The team used that money to "develop a plan that creates impactful visitor experiences, connects with a modern audience, and better reflects the diversity of our community both past and present."[1]

The grant allowed the museum to do further visitor research, revealing that many of its visitors were struggling with what the village was. Frontline staff were asked for their ideas and feedback in small and large group meetings. The working group also hosted a meeting for the entire board and all of the scholars involved with the project. In an effort to better present diverse histories, the working group engaged outside scholars and educators, and built relationships with universities. Each consultant helped them look at where the thematic holes were in the museum's interpretation. The group also looked for institutions that were doing interesting work. This resulted in a visit to Strawbery Banke, a living history museum in New England undergoing similar challenges. The project was not an effort to throw out or change everything but to look at how the museum could do better. The end result was a multi-year plan entitled *Foundations of Interpretation*. The new plan provides a path for Old Sturbridge Village to update written interpretation guides; develop purposeful learning, emotional, and social targets for programs and exhibitions; expand training programs; and improve interpretation signage.[2]

In August 2020, Old Sturbridge Village received $250,000 to fund an implementation grant. The second grant enables the partnership with the International Coalition of Sites of Conscience to focus on training in diversity, equity, accessibility, and inclusion work, as well as dialogue-based interpretation. The grant will also support the revision of written interpretation guides for 37 spaces. This will help the museum move beyond just delivering content to helping interpretive staff facilitate meaningful dialogs with visitors. Finally, the plan calls for the creation of signage for structures and locations throughout the museum that will help visitors navigate the museum campus.[3]

IMPLEMENTING THE INTERPRETIVE MASTER PLAN IN DAY-TO-DAY PROGRAMMING

Old Sturbridge Village has found that time is the biggest challenge to implementing their interpretation plan during the COVID-19 pandemic. Written to support what was already happening organically, the new plan ties into everything. The planning grant solidified these ideas, committing OSV to become the museum to which it aspired. The implementation grant builds on that. Change is always challenging. Nevertheless, Old Sturbridge Village has persevered and found a way forward, despite a global pandemic.

Old Sturbridge Village's board will not be asked to officially approve the new interpretive plan. This is in keeping with previous interpretive planning efforts at the museum. The leadership team is depending on staff buy-in to ensure the plan's success.

ADVICE TO OTHER ORGANIZATIONS UNDERTAKING AN INTERPRETIVE MASTER PLAN

When asked what advice she would give colleagues considering embarking on an interpretive master plan, Avenia said, "The museum field is special. Call others who have gone through this planning process. Talking to institutions like or not like your own is immeasurably helpful. It is a daunting process, don't go it alone."[4] She goes on to encourage fellow museum professionals to be flexible, citing the pandemic as an example of an outside force that can really cripple, even destroy, your project if you aren't able to think outside of the box when necessary. Furthermore, Avenia points out how the success or failure of a plan depends on excellent communication.

NOTES

1. National Endowment for the Humanities, "Funded Projects Query Form," accessed November 20, 2020, https://securegrants.neh.gov/publicquery/main.aspx?f=1&gn=BP-261032-18.

2. Old Sturbridge Village, "Old Sturbridge Village Annual Report, Fiscal Year 2020" (2020), 9, accessed November 30, 2020, https://www.osv.org/about/visitor-magazine-annual-reports/.

3. Ibid.

4. Interview with Caitlin Emery Avenia, November 19, 2020.

Appendix F

'Iolani Palace

Founded: Opened as museum: 1978

Location: Honolulu, Hawai'i

Mission Statement: E malama, hoihoi hou, wehewehe, kaana a hoohiwahiwa i ke ano laha ole o ka moomeheu, ka moaukala a me ka mana o ka Hale Alii o Iolani a me kona pa no ka pono o ke kanaka oiwi a me ka poe o Hawai'i nei a me ko ke ao nei (To preserve, restore, interpret, share, and celebrate the unique cultural, historical, and spiritual qualities of 'Iolani Palace and its grounds for the benefit of native Hawaiians, the people of Hawai'i, and the world).

Target Audiences:
- Native Hawaiians, all people of Hawai'i, and visitors to Hawai'i
- Traditional and non-traditional families, children, and caregivers
- Two special audiences: multigenerational families, school-based audiences

Themes: 'Iolani Palace functioned as the heart of the Kingdom of Hawai'i and a hub for the Pacific region while simultaneously seeking to demonstrate Hawai'i's stature in the Western world. It straddled a period of political instability, caught between cultures. Its many expressions of creativity, such as food, music, dance, and entertainment demonstrated both the duality and the convergence of native and non-native influences, old ties, and new aspirations.

Secondary/subthemes:
- The story of 'Iolani Palace is set against a background of international empire-building, a time of great tension for the Hawaiian monarchy as it sought to retain the nation's independence from foreign dominance and to assert its leadership in the Polynesian world.

- Throughout his reign, King Kalakaua sought to build international connections and to demonstrate Hawai'i's sophistication and leadership in the contemporary world.
- In addition to courting international recognition, King Kalakaua promoted, revived, and highlighted traditional Polynesian and Hawaiian culture, celebrating and reviving his nation's unique heritage.
- The cultural and social life of the palace illustrated how Hawai'i had become a crossroads of commerce and a center for the convergence of international and domestic tastes, styles, cultures, and people. The crossroads influences are profoundly evident in music, cuisine, and celebration.
- The political and personal tragedies that occurred at the palace shaped its future, as well as public sentiment in the decades that have followed. Today it remains a symbol of Hawaiian history, culture, resilience, and hope.

Interpretive Master Plan Completed: April 2014

On the museum website, 'Iolani Palace is referred to as "a living restoration of a proud Hawaiian national identity." The museum description continues by using words like spiritual, epicenter, and sacred for the palace and its grounds. The description does not exaggerate; not only was 'Iolani Palace the only official royal residence in the United States, it was the home to Hawai'i's last monarchs and the site where the United States overthrew the Hawaiian monarchy in 1893.

In writing 'Iolani Palace's interpretive master plan, author Beverly Sheppard states, "We know that collections and their stories, galleries and their design, and content and its interpreters are the catalysts for discovery."[1] Written as a five-year plan, the document defines audience and institutional goals for the site and connects the museum's exhibits, programs, and visitor services to the essential themes that form the base for telling the palace's unique story. 'Iolani Palace started its journey toward the interpretive master planning process with a Museum Assessment Program (MAP) and an audience study in 2009. Both projects challenged the historic site to explore new avenues of interpretation and programming that were relevant to current audiences and to incorporate a broader range of interpretive techniques.

The resulting plan defined audiences, themes, and identified interpretive approaches for the different public spaces. The two audiences defined were multigenerational and school audiences. These audiences would be engaged by the overarching theme and five secondary themes listed above.

The interpretive approaches identified by the plan included "big picture" ideas that allowed for plenty of flexibility on the part of staff in determining docent-led tours and audio guides, traditional exhibits, a website including ideas links to related sites, teacher packets, online exhibits, podcasts, games and resources for children, and opportunities for guests to share their photographs of the palace.[2]

IMPLEMENTING THE INTERPRETIVE MASTER PLAN
IN DAY-TO-DAY PROGRAMMING

The director of curation and education, Teresa Valencia, started working at 'Iolani Palace in 2016, almost two years after the interpretive master plan was written. Not a native Hawaiian, she considers herself a project manager. When it comes to developing programs, she feels that the community voice should be front and center. Valencia doesn't see much written on how to involve community in the current interpretive master plan. That said, she feels that the plan has helped her in writing grants and program planning. While Kama'aina (locals) are not called out directly, the interpretive plan helps support museum efforts to develop school and family programs for the local community. In fact, it has acted as an outline for program development. She refers to it to refresh her memory. 'Iolani Palace now offers a First Sunday Families program with hands-on activities and more immersive spaces. Toddler kits, which asks families to work together to find shapes and colors in the palace, are popular. In fact, Valencia enjoys using them with her own three-year-old child.

Another area where Valencia has utilized the foundation set for the museum in the interpretive master plan is docent training. She works to incorporate the document's concepts into these trainings and finds that this ongoing training does serve to enhance docent knowledge.

One area where the interpretive master plan has proved to be very helpful is in defending her choices for program development to her board. It is also helpful in grant writing.

ADVICE TO OTHER ORGANIZATIONS UNDERTAKING
AN INTERPRETIVE MASTER PLAN

Because she was not part of the planning process for 'Iolani Palace's interpretive master plan, Valencia offers the unique perspective of a staff person who inherited her predecessors' vision. The 2014 plan was supported by input from an extensive 2009 audience survey and MAP review, but that input is now over 10 years old, and Valencia recognizes that the community's needs have expanded. She continues to use the plan she inherited, but recognizes that the need of both 'Iolani Palace and the community have evolved since it was written. Specifically, she'd like it to incorporate more social justice issues. The 'Iolani Palace functions as the heart of the Hawaiian kingdom, demonstrating Hawai'i's stature in the world. Valencia reads the current plan and feels it is written in colonial context. She sees a need to reach out to Kama'aina even more firmly in order to ensure that they see the palace as a space that remains fundamental to their community.[3]

NOTES

1. Beverly Sheppard, *Interpretive Plan for 'Iolani Palace* (Honolulu, HI: April 2014), 2.
2. Interview with Teresa Valencia, August 13, 2020.
3. Ibid.

Bibliography

"About the Denver Evaluation Network." Denver Evaluation Network. Accessed October 28, 2019. http://www.denverevaluationnetwork.org/about.html.

"About Winterthur." Winterthur Museum, Garden and Library. Accessed January 1, 2020. http://www.winterthur.org/visit/about-winterthur/.

Alderson, William T., and Shirley Payne Low. *Interpretation of Historic Sites*. Nashville, TN: American Association of State and Local History, 1982.

American Alliance of Museums. "Core Documents." AAM Ethics, Standards, and Professional Practices. Accessed August 28, 2019. www.aam-us.org/programs /ethics-standards-and-professional-practices/core-documents/.

———. "Developing a Strategic Institutional Plan." AAM Alliance Reference Guide. 2018. https:/www.aam-us.org/wp-content/uploads/2017/12/Developing-a-Strategic -Institutional-Plan-2018.pdf.

———. "Mission Statement. AAM Ethics, Standards, and Professional Practices. Accessed October 15, 2019. https://www.aam-us.org/programs/ethics-standards -and-professional-practices/mission-statement/ .

———. "Museum Assessment Program." AAM Accreditation and Excellence Programs. Accessed September 19, 2019. https://www.aam-us.org/programs/accredi tation-excellence-programs/museum-assessment-program-map/.

American Association of Museums. *National Standards and Best Practices for U.S. Museums.* Washington DC: AAM, 2008.

Andrew Merrill and Associates. *The Cumbres and Toltec Scenic Railroad Interpretive Master Plan*. April 2010.

Banas, Derek. "How to Find Demographics." New Think Tank. August 30, 2010. https://www.newthinktank.com/2010/08/how-to-find-demographics/.

Bell, Ashley. "Boost the Productivity of Your Meetings with These 26 Icebreaker Games." *Snacknation*. May 9, 2019. https://www.snacknation.com/blog/boost -productivity-meetings-icebreakers-games/.

BetterEvaluation. "Institutional Histories." 2011. https://www.betterevaluation.org /en/plan/approach/institutional_histories.

The Boudreaux Group, John Veverka and Associates. *Clemson University Interpretive Plan.* March 2017. https://www.clemson.edu/about/history/taskforce/documents/Report-3-10-2017.pdf.

Braden, Donna R. *Spaces that Tell Stories: Recreating Historical Environments.* Lanham, MD: Rowman & Littlefield, 2019.

Brochu, Lisa. *Interpretive Planning: The 5-M Model for Successful Planning Projects.* Ft. Collins, CO: National Association of Interpretation, 2014.

California State Parks System. *Interpretation Planning Workbook.* Sacramento, CA: 2013.

Carter, James (Ed.). *A Sense of Place: An Interpretive Planning Handbook.* Scottish Interpretation Network, 2001. https://portal.uni-freiburg.de/interpreteurope/service/publications/recommended-publications/carter_sense-of-place.pdf.

Chesapeake Bay Office, Northeast Region National Park Service. *Interpretive Planning Tools for Heritage Areas, Historic Trails and Gateways.* July 2010. https://www.nps.gov/subjects/heritageareas/upload/Interp-Planning-Toolkit-for-Heritage-Areas-Historic-Trails-and-Gateways-2.pdf.

Ciarlo, Giovanni. "Group Facilitation—A Step-by-Step Guide." *Gaia Education* (blog). August 18, 2017. https://medium.com/@gaiaeducation/group-facilitation-a-step-by-step-guide-b55495b057aa.

Colbert, Leonor A. "Practiced-based Perspectives on the Interpretive Planning Process." Master's thesis, University of Washington, 2017. https://digital.lib.washington.edu/researchworks/handle/1773/39766.

Cumbres and Toltec Scenic Railroad. "About Us." Accessed June 25, 2020. https://cumbrestoltec.com/.

Cumbres and Toltec Scenic Railroad Commission. "Mission Statement." Accessed June 25, 2020. http://commission.ctsrr.com/about/.

"Demographics." Investopedia, September 29, 2019. https://www.investopedia.com/terms/d/demographics.asp.

"Digital Collections." The Henry Ford. Accessed November 22, 2020. https://www.thehenryford.org/collections-and-research/digital-collections/artifact.

Falk, John, and Lynn Dierking. *The Museum Experience.* New York: Routledge, 2011.

Friends of the Cumbres and Toltec Scenic Railroad. "About Us." Accessed June 25, 2020, https://www.cumbrestoltec.org/about-us/mission.html.

Garecht, Joe. "6 Places to Find Grants for Your Non-Profit." The Fundraising Authority. Accessed Oct 1, 2020. http://www.thefundraisingauthority.com/grants/find-grants-nonprofit/.

Gartenhouse, Alan. *Minds in Motion: Using Museums to Expand Creative Thinking.* San Francisco: Caddo Gap Press, 1991.

Hague, Stephen G., and Laura C. Keim. "Budgets and Funding Interpretive Planning." *Small Museum Toolkit* (blog), December 19, 2012. http://smallmuseumtoolkit.blogspot.com/2012/.

Haley, M. K. "What's Brainstorming All About?" In Peggy Van Pelt (ed.), *The Imagineering Workout by Disney Imagineers.* New York: Disney Editions, 2005.

Hallgren, Larissa Hansen. "Interpretive Plans: The Spirit of a Museum." Larissa Hansen Hallgren. Accessed December 10, 2019. https://larissahansenhallgren.com /interpretive-plans-the-spirit-of-a-museum/.

HDC International. "The Veverka Interpretation Planning Process." Accessed November 9, 2020. https://www.heritagedestination.com/hdc-training---veverka -interpretation-planning-process/.

Heathfield, Susan M. "What Facilitation Is and How It Is Useful to Employers." The Balance Careers. Accessed June 25, 2019. https://www.thebalancecareers.com/what -is-facilitation-1918129.

Institute of Museum and Library Services. "IMLS Funds New and Improved Assessment Program for Small, Mid-Sized Museums." Accessed September 19, 2019. https://www.imls.gov/news/imls-funds-new-and-improved-assessment-program -small-mid-sized-museums.

John Milner Associates. *Silos and Smokestacks National Heritage Area Interpretive Plan.* Spring 2003. https://www.silosandsmokestacks.org/wp-content/uploads /2013/07/InterpretivePlan_complete.pdf.

Lewis, William J. *Interpreting for Park Visitors*. Philadelphia: Eastern National Park and Monuments Association, 1980.

Museum Galleries Scotland. "Planning Your Interpretation." Accessed February 15, 2020. https://www.museumsgalleriesscotland.org.uk/advice/collections/planning -your-interpretation/.

NAIinterpret. "I Am An Interpreter." YouTube video. 3:00. August 18, 2014. www .youtube.com/watch?v=8kZe5NosGxo.

National Endowment for the Humanities. "Funded Projects Query Form." Accessed November 20, 2020. https://securegrants.neh.gov/publicquery/main.aspx?f=1 &gn=BP-261032-18.

National Park Service. *Comprehensive Interpretive Planning.* Fall 2000. https://www .nps.gov/subjects/hfc/upload/cip-guideline.pdf.

———. *Interpretive Planning Handbook.* Harpers Ferry Center, WV: U.S. Department of the Interior, 1982. http://npshistory.com/publications/interpretation/interp -planning-handbook-1982.pdf.

———. "National Heritage Areas: Community-Led Conservation and Development." Last updated March 15, 2019. https://www.nps.gov/subjects/heritageareas /index.htm.

———. *Planning for Interpretation and Visitor Experience.* Harpers Ferry Center, WV: U.S. Department of the Interior, 1998.

Nosek, Elizabeth J. State Historic Fund Education Grant. *Colorado Railroad Museum Interpretive Master Plan—Education,* 2018.

Nova Scotia Museum. "Executive Summary." *Interpretive Master Plan.* March 2009. https://museum.novascotia.ca/sites/default/files/inline/images/executive-summary .pdf.

———. "True Confessions about Interpretive Master Planning: An Interactive Session." Slide Share, May 2, 2015. https://www.slideshare.net/mags_x/true -confessions-about-interpretive-master-planning-a-presentation-by-the-nova-sco tia-museum-for.

Old Sturbridge Village. "Old Sturbridge Village Annual Report Fiscal Year 2020." Accessed November 30, 2020. https://www.osv.org/about/visitor-magazine-annual-reports/.

Osborn, Alex. *Applied Imagination: Principles and Procedures of Creative Thinking.* New York: Scribner, 1953.

Putt, Neal, and Sarah Slade. *Team for Preventive Conservation.* Rome: International Centre for the Study of Preservation and Restoration of Cultural Property (ICCROM), 2004. https://www.iccrom.org/sites/default/files/ICCROM_01_Team work_en.pdf.

Randazzo, Laura. "How to Teach Theme." English Teacher Help, Free Lecture Slides, High School Teacher (Vlog). LauraRandazzo.com, October 7, 2017. https://www.youtube.com/watch?v=Hwbwdj4mAiU.

Selby, Holly. "The Fine Art of Teamwork; Collaboration among Curators Is Aiding Many Museums. But Is It Aiding Art?" *Baltimore Sun*, December 12, 1999. https://www.baltimoresun.com/news/bs-xpm-1999-12-12-9912210366-story.html.

Sheppard, Beverly. *Interpretive Plan for 'Iolani Palace.* Honolulu, HI: April 2014.

Silvers, Dana Mitroff. "Using Improv Games to Foster Creativity and Collaboration." Design Thinking for Museums. January 27, 2014. https://designthinkingformuse ums.net/tag/icebreakers/.

Sklar, Martin A. "Yes, If." In Peggy Van Pelt (ed.), *The Imagineering Workout by Disney Imagineers.* New York: Disney Editions, 2005.

Tilden, Freeman. *Interpreting Our Heritage*, third edition. Chapel Hill: University of North Carolina Press, 1987.

U.S. Forest Service, Center for Design and Interpretation. *Interpretive Planning—Tool #2: Interpretive Plans*, Version 2. Golden, CO: USDA Forest Service, September 2014.

Veverka, John. *Interpretive Master Planning* (Boston: Museums Etc., 2011).

Wells, Marcella D. *Creating More Meaningful Visitor Experiences: Planning for Interpretation and Education.* Denver: U.S. Department of the Interior, Bureau of Reclamation, 2009.

Wells, Marcella, Barbara Butler, and Judith Koke. *Interpretive Planning for Museums: Integrating Visitor Perspectives in Decision Making.* Walnut Creek, CA: Left Coast Press, 2013.

Index

Page references for figures and tables are italicized.

About the Author

Elizabeth Nosek has spent a career immersing herself in museums and their work. From Delaware to Hawai'i, she has focused her attention on ensuring that the stories museums tell not only engage audiences, but help them relate to the world they find themselves in. Nosek has always taken the word "curator" seriously, acting as a steward for the stories told through the collections where she worked. Whether an interpreter at Old Sturbridge Village in Massachusetts, the senior curator of Collections and Education at the Historic Mission Houses Museum in Honolulu, Hawai'i, or the curator of Education and Exhibits at the Colorado Railroad Museum, Nosek has looked for the connections that tie us together as a community.

Nosek's career has provided her with innumerable opportunities. She has not only worked with a variety of collections, researched and produced exhibits on topics ranging from quilts to railroads, but has also worked for traditional, decorative art, railroad, and living history museums as well as historic houses presenting countless tours, demonstrations, and programs. Over the course of her career, Nosek has also convinced myriad tour guides to give up their "talk at and drag around" tours and replace them with tours that engage their visitors through relatable themes.

Holding an undergraduate degree in cultural anthropology from Hamline University in Minnesota, Nosek went on to obtain her masters in history and museum studies at the Cooperstown Graduate Program in New York. She is certified in Montessori preprimary education and has a certificate from Disney University in Guest Services. She has published articles in museum trade journals and presented at numerous conferences on topics including historic foodways, collaborative programming and exhibits, building interpretive manuals, and guest service approaches using company cultures such as those at the Walt Disney Company and the Winterthur Museum, Gardens and Library. Nosek has also consulted with other museums and organizations on food history, educational/interpretive programs, and visitor services.